DISRUPTION

The singular attitude of the falcon god means very much more than just an attendance on the pharaoh, the back of whose neck he covers and warms at the very sensitive spot which neurology calls the "Bridge of Varolius," which puts him into almost immediate contact with the cervical nerve ganglion that certain anatomists have named the "Tree of Life." Could it not be said that by means of this warm touch the divine Bird, symbol of the heart of the deity, in some way fecundates Chephren's spirit in the brain, in that hostelry where, according to the sages of that epoch, the thoughts conceived and born in the heart stay a while before they can be sent out into the world by the movement of the tongue and the opening of the lips, in the utterance of words?

—Louis Charbonneau-Lassay, *The Bestiary of Christ*

DISRUPTION

David Appelbaum

STATE UNIVERSITY OF NEW YORK PRESS

Cover: Khafre and the Horus-Falcon, black diorite veined with white, Dynasty IV, ca. 2558–2533 B.C., Cairo Museum, Egypt. Photograph
© G. Dagli Orti.

Published by
State University of New York Press, Albany

Printed in the United States of America

For information, address State University of New York Press,
State University Plaza, Albany, NY 12246

Production by Dana Foote
Marketing by Bernadette LaManna

LIBRARY OF CONGRESS CATALOGING-IN-PUBLICATION DATA

David Appelbaum.
Disruption / David Appelbaum.
p. cm.
Includes bibliographical references and index.
ISBN 0–7914–2797–8 (alk. paper). — ISBN 0–7914–2798–6 (pbk. : alk. paper)
1. Perception. 2. Consciousness. 3. Meaning (Philosophy)
4. Ethics. I. Title.
B945.A663D57 1996
121'.3—dc20 95-40494
CIP

10 9 8 7 6 5 4 3 2 1

CONTENTS

Introduction vii

PART I
PRELIMINARY COLLECTION

1 Instruments 3

The Blank of Mind 3
Inner Speaking 10
Inner Listening 12

2 Usages 19

Impressions 19
Perception of the Formless and Formless Perception 24
Two Digressions 30
Nirvikalpanic and Visayagatic Perception in Advaita Vedanta 30
On Visual Geometry 31
Recapitulation 33

PART II
TRANSITION TO MOVEMENT

3 Husserl and Internal Time Consciousness 39

4 Toward a Somatic Critique of Retentivity 45

5 The Betweenness of the Somatic Field 51

6 Digression on Projective Geometry 69

PART III
TRANSFORMATION

7 The Interval 79

8 Objectivity and Meaning 87

9 Sympathy and the Plight of the Self 95

DISRUPTION

10 "Becoming Similar" 103

11 Nondisclosure 111

PART IV
SUMMONS

12 Initiation 121

13 Suffering and the Passivity of the Subject 129

14 Effort and Praxis 137

15 Conscience 145

16 The Surpassing 153

Postscript. The Mighty 159

Notes 163

Bibliography 171

Index 175

INTRODUCTION

The human act is disrupted in initiation, motivation, and accomplishment. It is broken off before completion and left to express its imperfection through discourse and signification. Since its discontinuous character calls for redemption, the perennial temptation of a philosophy of being equates disruption with disintegration and devaluation and proceeds to eliminate the former. To rid ontology of an unruly force that commands an irradicable obedience has been a project of philosophy since the Enlightenment, probably since Aristotelean metaphysics.

What is the signification of that which disrupts the human act, particularly the act of signification?

The question itself is a force that shears off the play wherein consciousness reproduces the conditions of its own production, loss, and recovery, as well as its own obsessive aversion to disruption. To be in front of the question is to bring the automatism of self-interest to a stop and to face a matter different from any known.

Inasmuch as knowledge concerns what is, confrontation with the force of disruption requires, as a first step, the bracketing of ontology, of what Husserl calls the "space-time continuum." Like the gravitational pull of the earth, being draws consciousness to it, lending consciousness a ponderous weight that gives to an initial escape the thrill of an existential exclamation. Although the virtues of ground and horizon, both essential to ontology, are difficult to sacrifice, that which breaks into consciousness with a signification other than being promises movement and alteration. From the first taste, an altered consciousness in all its opacity clearly belongs to that which is higher. The vertical, hierarchy, and that which remains above follow from abandonment of being's transparent horizon.

Sacrifice of the for-itself, the self-legislating consciousness and apperception that seeks the upper limits to its knowing presence, seems initially to bear the mark of a barbarism. Do we not ask rhetorically, could there be a value higher than freedom and the memory that safeguards freedom? In the hesitancy of response, in the delay that keeps the sign from automatically signifying its signification, an enigmatic summons to subjectivity resounds. The subtlety of its command, juxtaposed with the coarse, insouciant ways of attendance, makes it remarkable that the call is ever heard. Nonetheless, its force of movement makes obedience imperative and refusal, an act of insubordination.

That which takes precedent to command a disruption to the free play of consciousness commands a responsibility. To be a responsible one is a commandment that predates one's birth, the origination of one's birth, and the origination of origination. Responsibility awaits the human subject as the air awaits the lungs, as life awaits the body, and as destiny awaits humanity. Inasmuch as the subject is given no recourse, responsibility chooses its subject like an abrupt tap on the shoulder. One's response measures and is measured by acceptance of the work.

The surpassing or that which takes precedence disrupts consciousness through the vehicle of the other's command. A tear-stained face, an outstretched palm, a broken and bleeding body, bones twisted by the torturer, blood coagulated by the executioner's instruments—neighbor, stranger, brother, sister, child—the other is other than self yet commanding through the self's own lips. The summons to awaken, dress wounds and uplift the other, is uttered by one not the same nor yet different from oneself. The absolute gap that yawns between one and the other—within subjectivity—is bridged by the ethical command that knows neither time nor space, relative nor absolute, self nor other.

As I speak of it, ethical obligation is not an achievement or attainment (since it is not a choice) but an obedience to that which disruptively commands us to obey. Because the ethical does not consist of "doing" but undoing, no particular undertaking is certain to fulfill the conditions of obligation. Certainty itself is a feature of the for-itself that constitutes itself through acts of intentionality that carry a force of certitude, whereas the ethical is fraught with risk, vagueness, and the exceptional. The quest to meet the fact of obligation involves phantom hopes and illusory successes as the debris of demagoguery and fascism vividly prove. Unless one is an initiate into the work of the ethical, a self-instigated calm of consciousness restores the seamless play before any disruptive break is recognized—if totalitarian and eternalistic dreams have not already gained ascendence. An ethics without initiation lacks the anarchaic and anarchic force with which to wake the sleep of being.

Initiation supposes a guidance other than consciousness and implies a knowledge other than the self-constituted principles of the "I think." Rejection of an initiatic approach, whether sceptical or otherwise, restricts knowledge to the ego, empirical or transcendental. Since knowledge is given by the same laws to each separate subject, knowledge is the same. An epistemology of sameness draws itself up into an ethics of despair with a resigned shrug of the shoulders.

Other than consciousness, a guide disturbs and profoundly ruptures the matter of awareness, confronting it with alteration and movement. The autonomous play that serves an obsessive fear of disruption abruptly ends, and contact and contiguity disclose the other in proximity, as already touching the body from inside. The sympathetic, nonthematizable response to that touch incarnates the living basis of the ethical. Through the touch, the other categorically and disruptively commands, and though I will speak of it throughout this study, its utterance is fundamentally oracular and divinatory. Translation back into speech—which is a speaking of being, an ontological language—erases difference with the hand of sameness.

Why say that ethics is not a matter of reason, judgment, and deliberative choice, as a broad tradition has argued? Why agree with Dostoevsky's words that describe the ethical as "all that is exceptional, vague, and enigmatic"?

The tolerance that consciousness has for disruption, its elasticity and denial, is exemplified in its love of continuity. A break, gap, hiatus, or caesura in its discourse is forthwith examined by means of the discursive, converting what was other than consciousness back into the cipher of speech. So great is the resiliance of discourse that it is able to blanket the world with a seamless fabric, bringing all that there is into its folds. The vast project of tradition, to make human discourse the shepherd of being (Heidegger), is, beneath it all, an expression of the tolerance I spoke of. That tolerance is a political virtue and that ontology serves a political aim are implications that I will not further discuss.

To locate the ethical within the frame of discourse of consciousness is to dislocate it from the disruptive other. It is also to replace obedience and responsibility, keynotes of the ethical, with freedom, an ontological mode extrapolated from the free play of consciousness. That which takes precedence by virtue of being higher than humanity is thereby cut off from contact with human subjectivity. Since the subject's lack of potentization goes unaddressed, a full and balanced development of subjectivity is precluded and he or she can become only more of the same. The plight of our present ontological epoch (now nearly three millenia old) is captivity by essence, conformity, the relative, the cultural.

It is the other in front of me—neighbor, friend, enemy, stranger—that disrupts production of the space-time continuum with the exigence of his or her situation and commands in a categorical voice: that I help. Not to obey, to refuse responsibility, to retreat to the position of free choice, is an act of insubordination. That I am fully capable of allowing consciousness "to knit up the raveled sleeve of care" is proof that the advent of the ethical is by force. A violent intercession, an exception to the rule of law that is anarchic and anarchaic, the disruptive other gives no option other than to be disrupted by the other's exigence and to face the uncertain potentization it implies.

To follow the guide of disruption is to follow no master other than the subject's responsiveness to the exigent other. If the ethical had masters, a slavish attitude would deprive followers of induction into the enigma of obedience. Mastery of that which in subjectivity is able to meet the face of disruption with a compassionate heart speaks of the initiatory way. Open to all, that way is walked in the shoes of perplexity, inadequacy, and courage until, worn through, the impediments to initiation fall away.

Since to face my fellow human being as disruptive brings me face to face with my lack and privation of response, I am initiated through the milieu of the absent. Through contact, the mystery of exchange is reenacted whereby I give my place to the other and take the other's place for myself. Trading places, I put on the dress of the other's suffering, and partake in the movement that can cross the unbridgeable gap between the one and the other. The act of obedience is not strictly for relief or palliation of the other, but for transmission of a memory that elevates both our conditions. Remembering the higher in which the one is for the other and the other for the one, I initiate the act that gains me entry into the ethical.

Through praxis, the subject recurs to the higher and is remembered to a memory without origin or principle. The gradual or sudden incarnation of the memory is conscience. By conscience, one is initiated into the mystery that is conscience. My essay, in its disruptive guise, concerns the development of an "organ" other than consciousness, that has on occasion been given the name of conscience.

Through contact, one meets the other whose infinite separateness poses both threat and promise. The promise is in the safety of indifference, the distance of noncommitment and dysrelation—which is quickly translated into transparent space filled with light. The threat is disruption. Existing beyond one's autonomous sphere, the other breaks exigently into consciousness, "full of sores and strife." The meeting, moreover, does not take place on neutral territory but on terrain alien to the for-itself and its interests—in the soma.

What is other than consciousness wears the clothes of life, its body. Since awareness of soma appears as the first alteration of consciousness, the shift to a consciousness *of* the other, and then to a consciousness *as* the other, takes place in the body, sensitivity, the circulation of hyletic material (Husserl), the subtle body. An altered configuration of soma, under the influence of the higher, confers agency of an ethical kind. Remembering what takes precedence does not proceed by theme and reflection, but by a logos unique to the body, one able to respond to the alogical command of the other.

Since to turn attention to the somatic initiation of movement is a praxis, the kind of practice I have in mind could be called a "body praxis." Since the body itself is vehicle of initiation, sensitive to the command of inner transformation, the development of conscience and the ethical as a whole follows a body praxis. If Spinoza meant this when he wrote, "He who possesses a body capable of the greatest number of activities possesses a mind whereof the greatest part is eternal," then my thought is congruent to his [*Ethics* V.39].

Since the door to the other opens inward, the spell of the outer figure who is other—which is projection, obsession, and self-interest—must be broken. That xenophobic spell paralyzes ethical agency and mesmerizes subjectivity with problems of knowledge (how to know other minds), choice (how to calculate utility), or life (why not to suicide.) The abrupt dispelling of the apparition of the other at the same time prefigures a memory of the ethical. Since to take the other in and give the other my place is to be reconfigured by the higher, calculation of need itself must be sacrificed by the gesture of reaching across the gap and touching the other's open sores. In touch, a memory not borne in memory floods consciousness and awakens remembrance of a forgotten obedience.

Because contact and sensitivity speak a speech different from intellect, the present work offers an approach other than that of a tradition of intellectualism. Although a nonconceptual, somatic praxis may seem unpracticable, once the prejudices of indifference drop and continguity recurs, the mysterious exchange whereby the one and the other trade places becomes a matter of intense practical concern. Although abandon and relaxation as effort reveal one's intellectualist assumptions, they are nonetheless operative factors in the exercise of subjectivity.

If to place the present work within an intellectualist tradition is to misplace it, to what tradition does it belong? The mistake of intellectualism should not be replaced by that of traditionalism since the rupture of consciousness not only eschews tradition per se but even precipitates a disruption or destruction of tradition. That force can no more be confined by the rules of confinement within a tradition than can air by my fist.

A-traditional or antitraditional, the signification of disruption predates being and perpetually intervenes in the perfect fit between sign and signified. The past to which disruption belongs is more ancient than that of the spiritual tradition of the West (with its keynote of ontology), more remote even than the ancestors worshipped by that tradition. Since that past has never been present, it is intransigent to representation. Neither can the concept, itself shucked from the core of being, grasp a past more remote than any tense. Disruption belongs to that which was there to meet thought, whenever thought was born—just as the sea met Love at Love's birth. The nakedness that thought clothes, disruption undresses and leaves speechless.

I speak of a philosophical work that has no history, continuity, or culture—yet commands that it be spoken! Although to the order and organization of thought, this work juxtaposes anarchy and dysfunction, its claim to the highest rigor is not empty. If rigor is not set equal to rigidity, it carries the sense of precision in movement. The rigor of deontological work of the present species consists of setting thought in movement in a precise direction—initiation into the higher. If tradition equals orthodoxy and disrupted tradition equals heresy, then that which I examine is philosophically heretical. The danger is that, becoming a position, it loses the rigorous signification of the ethical, and quickly becomes part of the resilient net of beings that keeps being sequestered from what takes precedence.

Expression of the ethical is subject to danger on every side. Nihilism (denial of the ethical) and eternalism (ontologization of the ethical) are the Scylla and Charybdis through which expression must pass. Stoicism, epicureanism, and utilitarianism, to name a few, are vessels that have floundered on the clashing rocks. Since Nietzsche decried the perils of nihilism over one hundred years ago, our wariness of the subtle serpent of denial has grown. Although we are still tempted by it, the greater tempter is eternalism. In a time that seeks the solace of spirit, nothing comforts like ontology with its promise of peace. What could be of more inestimable value? Yet while the way beyond eternalism is war, strife, and conflict—the never-at-rest disruption—it is that work that truly commands and is commanded by the higher. Toward that pitch the present work is directed.

My study is bivocal, possibly polyvocal. An unpremeditated shift in voice occurs near the start of the second part, in the section concerning Husserl's conception of internal time. Prior to the break, the effort is to continue a critique of Enlightenment views of perception, begun in an earlier work (*The Stop* [David Appelbaum, State University of New York Press, 1995]). The point is to articulate the role of tension (retention, intention, attention, detention) in eighteenth-century theory of knowledge, with the aim of exposing the intellectualist position. This tradition since Plato's time has favored theme and transparency over an unthematized opacity, that is, concept and representation over sensitivity. Its preoccupation with ontological disclosure has disposed it to relegate perception to the service of cognition and to eliminate any noncognitive residue.

After the break, the focus moves beyond a consciousness with intellectual predispositions. As an initial step toward an altered consciousness, I consider a "somatic critique of retention" that uncovers sympathy as constituent of awareness. A sympathetic form of perception that involves the lived-body experience avoids the pitfalls of a cognitively endowed outlook. The third part attempts to work out the basis of meaning within the horizon of an essentialistic approach to consciousness and to offer a critique of essentialism. The fourth part develops the implications of a consciousness whose recognition is based not on the ontological but the ethical. Both parts center on a memory whose vagrancy interferes with the automatic function of mind and whose force indicates a consciousness higher than our own.

No thought exists in isolation. All thought is related by its nature both horizontally and vertically. I wish to acknowledge the impetus to the present work given by Stephen David Ross whose questions on *theoria* and whose reference material, graciously supplied, helped my thought find its way. Since the Greek *theoros* was a witness sent to observe religious rituals and report back to the presidium, the question of attesting to the philosophical commitments behind the "ritual" of the stop was enormously stimulating. William Eastman, of the State University of New York Press gave courage and support to all stages of the project. The germ of the idea was presented me by William Segal and Margaret Flinsch. Above all, the support of my family, throughout the disruption of my disappearance, made this work possible.

I

PRELIMINARY COLLECTION

ARGUMENT

Object consciousness as a mode of awareness imposes an economy on the workings of our human resources. It is an economy bent on production, hyperactive and tyrannical. It is geared toward prevention of stoppage, and so, is ever vigilant toward possible disruption. The retentive character (first named by Locke) is self-frustrating in that its production of objects expends more than it yields. Under the hand of retention, things inevitably run down. In the dilemma (Hume's) that thought is already enervated, derivative, and deanimated at its birth, the absolute difference of somatic awareness presents itself. That which disrupts intellectual production arises within the soma, hidden beyond the frame of the object. Noncognitive, this kinaesthetic movement—sensation itself—is opaque and therefore disruptive to the light-embued gaze of intellect. Within the absolute difference of somatic awareness, the *arche* name *I* is sound—to constitute difference itself. Thus ends the impersonal term of sameness only under which can object production proceed.

1

INSTRUMENTS

THE BLANK OF MIND

My mind draws a blank. How to remember her name? Her scent I can almost smell, her face I can picture (red hair, high cheekbones, sad, green eyes), the way she speaks (accent, intonation, tempo) comes back to me. I recall the last time we met, the restaurant (on High Street?), and how we spoke about Mount Athos. But her name? It is on the tip of my tongue. My lips are ready to form its sound. . . . Nothing comes.

Mnemonics fail to break the grip of amnesia. The blank remains, stalling me. It is a gap, a tangible nothing that in turn creates an amnesia of intention. It is a hole in the seamless wall that holds back chaos. It is a power whose destabilizing effect translates to the constellation of meanings—my world. My mind *is* a blank and I mind only it. Thought and action, stopped in their trajectories, cease to be meaningful continuities. Their geometry disfigured, they fall under the category of zero. Unfinished, incomplete, bearing no marking, vacuous, signifying nothing, empty, devoid of purpose or hope, barren, fruitless. The whole field of signification is under seige. The blank betokens a danger.

A danger? The blank? One would like to believe the blank signifies merely a minor breakdown (like that minimalist notion, the glitch) in the otherwise smooth operation of mind, a hiccup, a slight dysfunctionality, a situational abnormality, a bug in the works. Loss would be confined to a few bytes and order easily restored. Such is the dismissive attitude of a cool hour when the blank has been neutered, reified, conceptualized, reduced to a colorless, secondary role in discourse. Why make a scene of not remembering a name?

DISRUPTION

In the heat of the event (Damn, I remember she was a friend of Harry's and liked reading May Sarton), knowledge is fundamentally constrained. Surprisingly, Locke is first aware of the fundamental difficulty. In an important section of the *Essay Concerning Human Understanding* entitled "Of Retention," he alludes to the blank's deep threat to intellect. The section deals with memory, essentially an act of interior gazing—of "viewing again." Once an idea has been "fixed" by attention and repetition, the "eye of the soul" is able to locate it in its field of vision. Gazing has its vulnerabilities, affection for instance. Emotional disturbance suddenly frees a memory or alternatively eclipses a clear reminiscence. Vulnerability in turn heralds two further aspects, each more fundamental than the former: gazing's teleology—to rouse "dormant ideas"—and its economy, retention. The last is the particular concern of the present chapter.

What is more threatening to a secret than exposure? Fear of coming out of closet or cave is a primal fear. Thus the blank's danger to Locke's deepest and most secret discovery—the *tentive* character of mind. It is a secret discovery because, never explicitly stated, tentivity is expressed in each of Locke's positions: a representational theory of meaning, principles of abstraction and induction, and a dispositional theory of ethics. It is the invisible hub around which these satellites turn, at the same time invisibly and eternally banishing its sole rival, recollection. It forms the deepest stratum because tentivity is his answer to one of the most ancient of problems. The question was already old when Aristotle asked it again: "why should the perception of the mere present impression be memory of something else, instead of being related to this impression alone?"[1] The question related to that of time: how does knowledge of the past arise when that which we know directly through experience is in the present? Aristotle in fact prefaces his remarks in *On Memory and Reminiscence* by listing the sole philosophical alternatives. He says that

> the persons who possess a retentive memory are not identical with those who excel in power of recollecting; indeed as a rule slow people have a good memory whereas those who are quick-witted and clever are better at recollecting.[2]

To grasp, grip, seize, hold, clutch, keep, secure, or retain describes *the* basic intellectual act of preservation. It is that through which the nonpresent, the absent, comes to be known. Preservation also has an obverse. Because of intellect's grasping, we cease to be available to the solicitation of the present. Tentivity is the cloak of concealment under which lurks the ultimate untenability of the position.

Locke's grand discovery of the retentive may have precipitated from the prevailing *episteme* like a crystal from a saturated solution. If to grope for origins by use of analysis and recombination of simple elements (for Locke, simple ideas) facilitates his discovery, the method also obscures its grandure. Retention is listed merely as a faculty of mind, a faculty among faculties—not, as it is, *the* faculty of faculties. In fact, retention organizes the whole economy of mind in such a way that, where it is not active, intellectual transaction and exchange, as we know it, grind to a stop. This fact does not emerge until a breakdown situation, when memory fails. "Memory in an intellectual creature," Locke says, "where it is wanting, all the rest of our faculties are in a great measure useless."[3] Retention becomes wealth, the power to extend beyond the immediately given. The equation is given even greater force in his second *Treatise of Government* where what one removes by one's own labor from what is common to all becomes one's property, the sole basis of wealth.

> Whatsoever then he removes out of the state that nature hath provided and left it in, he hath mixed his labor with and joined to it something that is his own and thereby makes it his property.[4]

Where retention is poor, when "we in our thoughts, reasoning, and knowledge, could not proceed beyond present objects," poverty results. The lack of intellectual grip signifies an impoverishment of power, estate, quality, and elevation as much as does lack of personal property. That lack supplies all the incentive necessary to drive an economy of retention. What Locke calls "perfect ignorance"—blankness—is to be avoided at all cost lest one lapse into slavery (poverty amongst wealth), dispossession, and presentness.

Recalling the inner dynamics, the infrastructure, of retentive memory, we need to fill a missing gap. An understanding of fear of poverty is necessary in order to explain the absolute rigidity attending the gaze—though up to a certain point, fear itself sharpens the wits. Think of it. Economically, it is a given that the gaze functions amidst wild, destabilizing forces. Each threat to blot out memory and displace time from the past—desire, pleasure, emotion, appetite, inapposite thought and imagery—must be overcome by an operation inherently reticent, delicate, meek, and reserved. The gaze, therefore, must be jealously guarded against dulling, stultifying influences that shrink its vital, expanding vision. A variety of controls can be exercised on an idea already in view (contemplation) or on an idea not yet observed but held ready for viewing. The latter (memory proper in Locke's terms) reaches toward an extreme point of vigilance, a hyperextension of vigilance. It must retain contact with potential memories, and even impossible ones that actually did take place. Our appreciation of such a severely channeled concentration grows.

There is more. With guardedness stretched to the limit by threat of blank global paralysis, retentivity is called to yet more drastic measures. They form the secret of Locke's secretness and spawn a host of special economic devices, including domination, subjugation, disfigurement, and marginalization. These techniques are directed toward the least impressive of all targets—the unmemorable, unremarkable, barely noticeable, trivializable, and inconsequential event. How are we to understand this remarkable watchfulness? Like low-flying aircraft, those phenomena that move below our line of vision pose the greatest threat. Unlike hordes of passions, hosts of desires, or armies of pleasure, they attack with no warning. They alone explain why the extensive regime of intellect remains on alert for discontinuity, blankness. Any break in the chain of command may bring instantaneous collapse, catastrope, defeat, death. Fear of a failed order of things is in the end fear of their mortal ruin.

Conversely, memory as retentive becomes an issue only after an episteme has become aware of threats to intellectual power. No such issue arises until intellect has come to power, as it did during the late Renaissance. Although retention is mentioned in the vast Aristotelean corpus, the Greek mind is not fully identified with the objectifying function of intellect. The decisive turn is taken with objectification of three-dimensional space, as typified in the rediscovery of linear perspective in art. Descartes, an early operator in the shift, transfers the whole human identity to the function. He does not yet, however, explicitly recognize its axis, choosing only to mention memory, "the practice of retaining the impressions for some time."[5] It is Locke's genius to perceive that an entirely new form of consciousness is based on retention. Just as a third dimension requires reorganized rules of spatial arrangement, so too object consciousness necessitates massively reorganized rules of exchange of energies within a human being. The new position of the intellectual function requires an increased power supply to execute its newly won authority. At the same time, the novel form of consciousness unmakes the work of that which preceeds it. Since to bind up the attention fully in intellectual pursuits is to cease to allow it to be harmoniously disposed to sensitivity and affectivity, a balanced awareness of reality is thereby superceded. Henceforth, consciousness will think its way to existence.

Locke grants only a glimpse of a preretentive condition. Prior to the hegemony of reason is the state of nature,

> a state of perfect freedom to order [people's] actions and dispose of their possessions and persons as they think fit, within the bounds of the law of nature, without asking leave, or depending upon the will of any other man.[6]

In the free economy, rules of exchange are established by relations of harmony. Rather than one aspect of consciousness vying against another for the attention, attentiveness belongs to the whole. Intellect, sensitivity, and affectivity coexist in equilibrium. The state of inner relatedness corresponds to a relatedness among persons. Such relations reflect the dynamics of inner exigence, to remain related in consciousness, to neutralize tendencies to separate, isolate, control, dominate. The state of nature is not, however, without conflict. Conflict in fact is a necessary phase in an equilbrium that moves toward integrity, disclosure, and freedom. The very movement forbids dwelling in conflict since it impedes a harmonious exchange essential to free attentiveness. Conflict exists as a state preceeding its own resolution.

Once a tentive principle is established, the older form of consciousness becomes a hypothetical reference point.

Locke adds mythic color to a description of the state of nature but little factuality; for example, "creatures of the same species

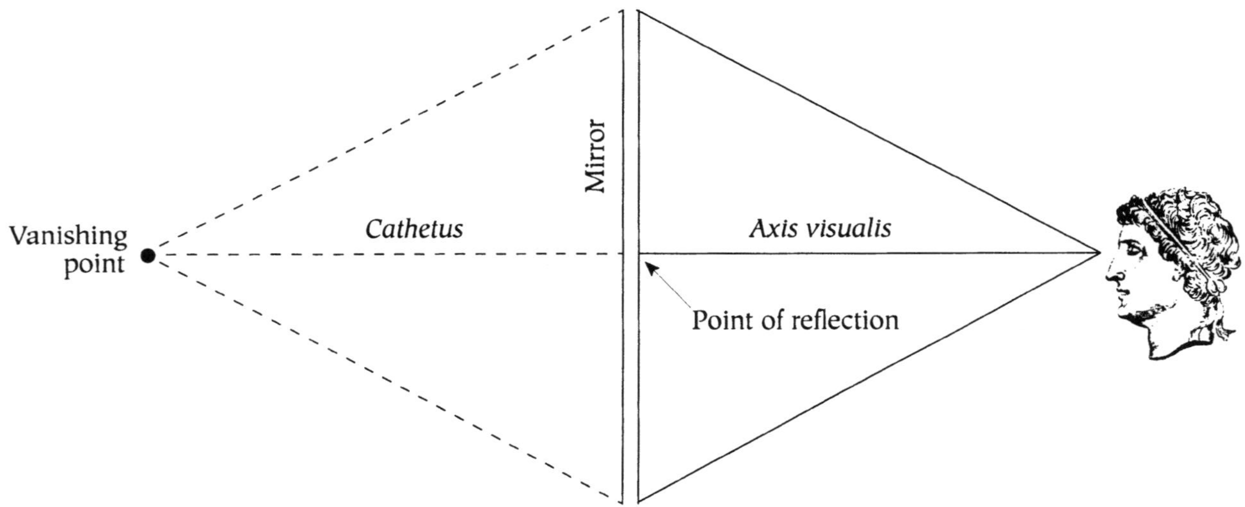
Vanishing point
Cathetus
Mirror
Axis visualis
Point of reflection

Figure 1

and rank, promiscuously born to all the same advantages of nature . . . should also be equal one amongst another. . . ."[7] In his epistemological thought, nothing at all is offered. Both works reveal what happens to consciousness under the gaze of retention. It becomes the vanishing point, the sightless eye that stares blankly back at the viewer—always unseen, yet always, like a black hole, drawing the vision gravitationally to it (figure 1).

Consciousness becomes the point of erasure that is everywhere and nowhere in the field of object consciousness. The point of decomposition, destabilization, displacement, disintegration of the object. The point that is nonisomorphic, that does not translate—the point that cannot be retained.

Because an idea unfolds in nonlinear time, adjacent points of intellectual history may be separated by epoches. So it is no surprise to find the twentieth century yields the next great student of retention and the blank of mind, Freud. In a chapter entitled "Forgetting of Proper Names" in the *Psychopathology of Everyday Life*, he notes the phenomenon of displacement:

> he who strives for the escaped name brings to consciousness others—substitute names—which, although immediately recognized as false, nevertheless obtrude themselves with great tenacity.[8]

The misremembered name (a displaced memory) serves supremely to fill in the blank (it obtrudes "with great tenacity") yet is obviously wrong. ("Mary." Why the hell do I remember "Mary" when that wasn't *her* name?) Its line of service can be traced, as Freud does in his own example, to reveal a "method" of avoidance, but not the form of consciousness avoided. The former avoidance strives invariably to conceal *thantos* or *eros*, death or sexuality. One name (the remembered one) covers over a second that has close associations with a forbidden subject. The forbiddenness has to do with the other measure of avoidance. Object consciousness strives mightily to conceal each point at which another consciousness might gain exposure. This striving, to be precise, is its tentivity. Forbiddenness awakens the striving.

Freud's advance over Locke is in designating the category of the forbidden. The forbidden is of indispensable value in retention since it must always be remembered if it is to be avoided. Its aura attracts the inner gaze the way a disquieting scene does the eye. The forbidden must always be resisted, shunned, repelled, annulled, and, therefore, retained in mind.

Freud's well-studied equation of the forbidden with the sexual gives an understanding of the retentive mechanism. The intellect's retentive gaze prevents an undesired spilling of seeds of knowledge.[9] It guards against profligate uses, retaining the germs to inseminate the understanding at the time of conception. Where ideas seep out, leak away, or are drained in pursuit of pleasure, a kind of will-less quiesence endangers thought. Postcoital *lethe* is the blank, "perfect ignorance," a small defect of intellect—minute, transient, but sufficient to bankrupt the state, rob the mind of its customary form of consciousness, and reinstitute an earlier, nonobjectifying form.

To retain is also to hold back in a continuous act of sacrifice. To suffer loss of pleasure is to offer up semen to a higher good, knowledge. To relinquish the discharge is to appreciate the usefulness of retention since memory empowers knowledge by preventing improper disemination of thought. Thought is celibacy and ascesis, a positing (not depositing) for the sake of accumulating mental force. Memory is that which cannot be sacrificed. Amnesia, temporary or not, is equivalent to depletion, impotence, flaccidity, detumescence—death in its sexual mode. Memory officiates the sacrifice of the free discharge of thought in order to preserve the species of consciousness it serves.

INNER SPEAKING

The blank places object consciousness on the altar of sacrifice. Who is to officiate? A most promising candidate refuses the role. The dangerous offering is banished beyond limits of intellect and civil society. The blank as erratum with no page number, as renegade with no real name. Visibly, there is no blank place in the field of objects. While the field is everywhere compact, the blank leaves its trace. Locke is thus not capable of total dismissal. Despite his attempt to minimalize it, the impress of the blank, incomplete and distorted, can be found in his text on language.

I am in the middle of a sentence, caught up with expression of thought. I come to the place where her name is to go . . . and it is blank! The vast machinery of discursive articulation grinds to a stop. Categorial selection, depth grammar, phonetic nuance, perceptual framing: all are suspended. In the stunning aftermath, the attention, momentarily freed from compulsive word production, can turn toward the context of discourse. The background of speech becomes audible only in the silence of speech. The background is not silence but, as Locke puts it, "articulate sounds," repeated subvocally. Nor is background accidental, a wayward nuisance or impediment to actual word production. Rather, inner speaking is a condition necessary for outer speaking, speaking plain and simple:

> Besides articulate sounds, therefore, it was further necessary that [one] should be able to use these sounds as signs of internal conceptions; and to make them stand as marks for the ideas within his own mind, whereby they might be made known to others, and the thoughts of men's minds be conveyed from one to another.[10]

The necessity of inner speech is the same as that of retentive memory. It is a necessity of constant rehearsal, practice and repetition of words—lest the technology fall idle. Idleness equals lethe and chaos; forgetting, losing one's grip, weakness of will. Idleness means slavery (not being able to appropriate property from nature) or the state of nature itself. Articulate sounds repeated subvocally alone immunize against muteness, "perfect ignorance." The force of necessity is measured by the blank and the turbulent wake it leaves. In an important section appropriately entitled, "Of the Imperfection of Words," Locke notes that "for the recording our own thoughts for the help of our own memories, whereby, as it were, we talk to ourselves, any words will serve the turn."[11] This is a stellar discovery. Sheer inner repetition of articulate sound serves an end other than that of making sense. Reason has good reason to take pains to conceal the fact; namely, that reasonableness itself is only a secondary property, a byproduct, the audible melody of a great underground cacophony. And that grating and grinding of gears finds its primary purpose in repeated continuation of the form of object consciousness. To perpetuate retentive memory, inner speaking came into being. Not for discourse but to keep engaged, like a flywheel, the mechanism of holding and grasping. Ungrammaticalities, semantic errors, nonsequitors, and perfect nonsense: linguistic fragments are strung end to end associatively—mixed in with occasional discursive thought—in order that the machinery run full time. The essential of language has nothing at all to do with discourse, though discourse pictures it otherwise. Discourse in a way is accidental, a throwaway discovery like Hermes's discovery of the tortoiseshell lyre. To speak of the absolute necessity of inner speech is to speak of that of productivity. Necessity is economic in character. Not to produce is to let the linguistic mechanism come to a stop.

And what would happen, should it stop? Whatsitsname?

The stream of inner speaking, the inner circuit of intellect communicating with itself, necessarily frames "civil" communication, persons speaking to one another. A modicum of focus gains possession of discourse, wrests it from the state of nature, and prepares it for exchange "about the ordinary affairs and conveniences of civil life, in the societies of men, one amongst another."[12] Antecedently, the subterranean babble, though constant and constantly inaudible, is not always the same. Retentivity affects level, density, dissonance, and intensity of inner speech while inner speech is the barometer of retentive pressure, recording fluctuations within a constant range. Receptivity to the inaudible has an opposite effect, penetrating as it were both constancy and necessity. To give ear to inner speech weakens the drive to produce words. At the same time, receptivity grows aware of both an absence of meaning and the cause of absence. The void of meaning is due to lack of an arche name, an I who speaks. No one speaks in inner speech, yet speaking inaudibly goes on. Because an I who speaks is missing from inner speech, it cannot be stopped—unless by an I who speaks.

INNER LISTENING

Under force of a blank moment, discourse dissolves to inner speech—a misnomer since such speaking lacks the semantic intent of discourse. "Communication of thoughts" is swallowed by obsession with utterance at a point between one word and the next. The new configuration is the same, with variations. Inner speech, like discourse, belongs to the tentive mind, in much the same way practicing scales and arpeggios belongs to the concert performance. The first is necessary to production of the second. One and the same mind is temporarily stunned "as by a gadfly" and brought to attention before its own productive activity, hence is different inasmuch as it experiences itself. Such experience is still peripheral, eccentric, from the outside, and barely related to anything other than objectification. Yet, the degree to which difference is acknowledged determines how the blank's specific potentiating powers affect knowledge. From within a point between two associative elements, inner speaking too can be tracelessly dissolved. Gradually or suddenly, speech is over. The inaudible monologue ceases to command the field and is swallowed, without a whisper, into the folds of another form of consciousness altogether. The call of the soma has been heard.

Dissolution of one field of consciousness (objectification) and eruption of a second (kinaesthesis). The event of transition, discontinuity, displacement, conversion, and metanoia is radical and complete. Subtle or explosive, it unmakes the impulse to produce meaning—and the whole semantic commentary on that which confronts the mind—and leaves . . . a gap.

The sequence I describe inverts an order endemic to Enlightenment tradition. Customarily, the second field is regarded as a degradation of the first. Degradation, deterioration, decomposition, loss. Conceptual meaning, product of sensory input, is framed within a state of ruin. Thought in any form is ruination. In this vein, Hobbes notices that "imagination therefore is nothing but *decaying sense*," and lawfully that "the longer the time is after the sight or sense of any object, the weaker the imagination."[13] Memory differs from imagination insofar as it takes time into account. The activity, whether memory or imagination, dwells in the contradictory tentive mind: object consciousness tries to grasp by repetition that which is ungraspable in uniqueness. That sensitivity inevitably decomposes to a deficient, desensitized condition speaks to a context of frustration, self-doubt, passivity, and paralysis—echoed in Hobbes's nasty and brutish description of the human condition. The attitudes accurately depict basic operations of the tentive mind: fixation of the attention, rigidification, stagnation, stuckness. It is from the character of these that the Hobbesian subtext arises.

The inversion I speak of is even clearer in Hume, though he lacks the clarity of Locke. A virtue of Hume's thought lies in its concreteness. Take a famous thought experiment of the *Inquiry*. I cite in full:

> Suppose therefore a person to have enjoyed his sight for thirty years and to have become perfectly ac-

> quainted with colors of all kinds, except one particular shade of blue, for instance, which it never has been his fortune to meet with; let all the different shades of that color, except that single one, be placed before him, descending gradually from the deepest to the lightest, it is plain that he will perceive a *blank* where that shade is wanting, and will be sensible that there is a greater distance in that place between the contiguous colors than in any other. Now I ask whether it be possible for him, from his own imagination, to supply this deficiency and raise up to himself the idea of that particular shade, though it had never been conveyed to him by his senses?[14]

Hume's interest is to demonstrate an exception to a basic insight: the absolute exclusiveness of impressions and ideas, "all our ideas or more feeble perceptions are copies of our impressions or more lively ones."[15] The exception occurs when in the midst of the color spectrum, a blank appears, a space between contin-guities or continuities. Hume remains unaware of an important subtext in the example and how it reveals his aversion. ["What's this color's name?"] Just like not remembering her name (I almost had it that time), Hume treats the absence as a slip of the mind. Though not a color, it is an almost-color, a spectral hue ("ghostly blue"), a place where color *should be*. It differs from colors on either side of it only by degree. It yields no radical separation since the missing shade can be interpolated, retrieved from memory. It is an equal that happens to be unequal (in acquaintance, in familiarity, in experience), and therefore not an abyss, a schism, an other—the blank. It is no real blank but one neutered, deenergized, and made computational. There is no decompression of the conscious field, no thrust of inversion, no echo of inner speaking, no blankness—nothing to raise the hairs on one's back. Here, the blank is no monster, no Cerebus, but appears in a sanitary, civil edition, expurgated for the tentive mind—a parody of itself. For Hume, the blank exists only in facsimile.

The blank and the inversion of consciousness. Consciousness appears as a higher form and inverts to a lower. Impression decomposes to idea, to thought. A lifelike but lifeless residue is left—one which no one would mistake for life. How to account for thought's inferiority to impressions—for isn't it this that drives

Hume to backgammon, skepticism, and despair? We need to read the subtext of the *Inquiry* deliberations. It is clear that awareness activated with an impression is more elevated, intense, and data rich because it is unproductive. Productivity, while essential to knowledge, is essentially a depletion, dissipation, and dispersal of energy. In itself, an impression can produce nothing. Evanescent, transient, ephemeral, it is an unimpeded energy complex, undisrupted movement, trace of a hidden signature, sign of an undeciphered symbol. Disrupted, it is no longer but in its place, another that is useful to know. The proto idea appears in the vapor trails of the impression. These mark, not consciousness of impressions, but death of that consciousness, its disintegration and loss of wholeness. That which is produced from the life of an impression is other than life, its Gorgon face, frozen in expression—enter, the representation.

Intellect arises in the privation I speak of. Object consciousness is directed toward replenishing an absent plenitude. It must forever erase the memory of that which it replaces. Production of objects of knowledge must, however, expend more—force, vitality, movement—than it yields. The end result takes the shape of an ignorance, if ignorance is that which chooses the lesser over the greater. It opts for scarcity over abundance. Uneconomical or antieconomical, the shift *ab initio* is to a losing concern. In defiance of free interchange, protectionist policies come into force. Boundaries are established, rules of commerce enforced, isolation established. These measures rigidify a plastic, dynamic condition, marked with vigor and vitality of exchange, in order to safeguard knowledge production. Like a law of self-evidence, the logic of productivity becomes inescapable. In the final stage, which is no different from the first stage, objectification renders control of production self-regulating and automatic.

The question of degradation detains Hume as little as it would one born to serfdom. "Gentle custom," an irony of nomenclature, is source of unyielding tyranny, a natural inevitability, a gravity, a centripetus, that overpowers consciousness of immediacy. Anything falling under its influence is brought down. Such is, as we have seen, the fate of the attention. An economy of thought chooses itself over that of sensitivity. Subjective necessity chooses itself over will, continuity over disruption, sameness over difference: choiceless automaticity! "This is the way things are done." Mechanicality defers asking after the coming-to-be, the origin, the ab-origin. Deference is a dislocation of Hume's perplexity concerning how an ephemeral impression differs from a stolid thought. The confusion is the postponement of a crisis. Between impressions and ideas yawns a gulf of consciousness marked "by their different degrees of force and vivacity." To neutralize a dangerous abyss, Hume resorts to the same device used successfully with the blank color. Picture a spectrum, not now of colors but of intensities. They form a rainbow of equalities, each incrementally congruent to its predecessor, all ordered by measurment. In the spectrum, a gap of consciousness is nonexistent in the same way a shade of blue is not missing. The difference between the two is invisible because difference itself is. What separates different forms *and* contents is not anything that can be named as different—gap toothed and barbarous. The separation cannot be bridged by the spirit of resemblance, that magical wand, whose power is to join impressions by affinity and similarity. Idea and impression are unlikes that resemblance cannot make alike. Even within the field of object consciousness, resemblance plays only a shadowy, deficient part.

Obscure to the nature of a shift in consciousness, Hume is forced to trumpet a new and impossible role for resemblance. Resemblance is recast as retentivity. Under the tutelage of this role, ideas are given the capability to "mimic or copy the perceptions of the senses." The labor of knowledge starts with xeroxing sensory information and goes into production from there. As critics from many schools have noted, only on the supposition of a privilege does tyranny gain a foothold. In this case, privilege belongs to a viewpoint that enables Hume to see what a perception in itself resembles. The innocence of resemblance thus becomes the wolf in sheep's clothing, for the viewpoint is none other than the gaze, at point-blank range. The gaze gazes retentively. Lo and behold, perceptual immediacy becomes productive, representational consciousness! To render experience memorable, the gaze annuls difference and opts for sameness of objectification.

While rimmed with confusions, Hume's peculiar lack of transparency suggests an advance of the question. Higher and lower, charged and depleted, impression and idea, are disjoined by difference unsympathetic to a logic of choice. The gap is there. It cannot be filled by a succession of likenesses comprehensible to a reason that then operates among them. Difference relates to neither one nor the other nor both nor either. It embodies a lack—of a principle of comprehension, of reason, of why *this* came into being, of what to do about it. In one consciousness's being degraded, the other is called forth. The higher, more active consciousness—of impressions—is crowned with immediacy and made up of "sensations or movements." It is unmodified by productive forces that impeded an unimpeded unfolding of awareness. From the arche name *I* to the world with which it communes, consciousness travels in contact with things, without loss—in the way sound fills a hall, bringing music to audience without audibly diluting itself. The image suggests how such an economy operates. A series of exchanges in which the pressure of the attention energizes and is energized by what it contacts maintains a level of "vivacity" that characterizes a higher consciousness. One thing is apparent to me in this image: that the utter transience of an impression is an accidental, not an essential feature of liveliness. A reciprocity of action such as described defines a community of beings through whose relations an energy level may be maintained.

The pathos of the disruption: "The most lively thought is still inferior to the dullest sensation."[16] Yet Hume remains fixed in a posture that forbids him from seeing the disruption for the pathos. Thus he unwittingly includes as elements of immediacy the contents of "when we hear or see, or feel, or love, or hate, or desire, or will."[17] The additions are not new configurations of energy, force, or power—basic percipience—but constructive or productive renditions of primary figures. They belong not to the raw and immediate but the processed and interpreted.

Knowledge born into a state of privation. Knowledge is impoverishment and deficit, energy crisis and depression. Knowledge keeps its intimacy with thanatos. All of these aspects come clearer when we see that an overstressed memory—a retentivity—comes to being simultaneous with loss. A blessing that belongs by right to the red twin is stolen away. The white twin, its thief, retains it. Jacob rather than Esau succeeds Isaac, Esau who by right of birth should. The rightful bloodline, vital, somatic, and silent, is cut short by deceit. Only the sickly pallor of thought, the cunning, contriving, manipulating line is victor. Thus is retentivity forever scarred, forever bent over to protect itself against a loss that, being coeval—*being twinned*—with itself, is irradicable in time.

DISRUPTION

Born deprived and depleted, object consciousness is spent before it begins. As Plato observes, the condition places it in relation to eros. *Je suis mort!* The productive intellect is discharge, enervation, sexual death. We can, on this ground, understand how Hume and other (male) figures come to view a disrupted consciousness from which thought descends by a stolen blessing. Immediacy is charged with erotic life. It is the turgid, preorgasmic condition, filled, liquid, labile, unattached to aspects of the field, improvizational, energic. All desirables but one have been cleared from the field. The summum bonum, the climax, gives a shape and consistency to perception and action. All lines of force point toward it; all lines of influence derive from it. To approach the source of definition is to allow a more fully articulate field. But approach is treacherous. Fullness of impression lies closest to an inevitable inversion, sudden and pleasurable collapse, discharge of energy, dyanmic of loss and retention—the blank. At the apex of sexual knowledge, at the peak from which one takes survey of all things, waits the blank. With the patience of a guerilla, it waits to void fullness, fluency, vitality, relation. And to leave . . . nothing.

2

USAGES

IMPRESSIONS

Concealment in the service of thought utilizes different categories: continuity, permanence, linearity, sameness. The astounding productivity of the enterprise—vast accomplishments of intellect, transfiguring the planet and spreading to cosmic space—casts a spell over all that is human, cradling and protecting it. Disruption is thereby disarmed. The stop, or its sibs, the blank, the gap, the gape, the lacuna, the caesura, the hiatus, the chasm, the hole, the canyon, the gulf, the abyss, are neutralized and erased—nearly. The blank suitable for intellectual form and provenance substitutes for an uneviserated and supervital blank lurking beneath. That this is so vouchsafes the power of object consciousness. It is immunized from disruption by an incredible foresight of mind, a hypervigiliance. Disruption anticipated, prelabeled, and watched for, is disruption that cannot wound. Thought could not exist without an early warning system. I am speaking of retentivity.

Anticipatory resoluteness is not infallable. A peculiar function of mind disruptively resurfaces. Nietzsche, alert to such traces, makes note of this anarchaic function, "this active oblivion." In a general way, it neutralizes retention. In relaxing the grip of the past, it is release, expansion, catharsis, and redemption. It undoes a compulsion to produce knowledge from immediacy, opens the channels to vital energy, cleanses the mind of expectation, and redeems the moment. Its appearance is desultory and without duration. It is the space between two thoughts.

Strangely, Nietzsche fails to capitalize on this bold discovery. Active oblivion does not, as we might expect, herald a break with object consciousness and a rapprochement with an awareness of a new level. The arc it subtends falls entirely on the productive mind. This is unexpected because *The Genealogy of Morals* purports to study the tentive character of mind and its expression of an intellectualized "morality." If we anticipate a disruptive power being ascribed to the "faculty of oblivion," Nietzsche's thought is bound to disappoint. That which is interrupted is inner speech in its capacity to interfere with productive thought. The faculty is charged with seeking "to introduce a little quiet into our consciousness so as to make room for the nobler functions and functionaries of our organism which do the governing and planning."[1] It is servant of intellect. Even stranger, it is lieutenant to an ethics of distress, aggression, and hopelessness.

This is a strange and strangely romanticized rendition of the anarchaic function. Active oblivion obliterates either too much or not enough. Not enough in that intellectual productivity increases; too much in that awareness of interior speaking is dulled. To restrict its purpose to ensuring "that what we experience and digest psychologically does not in the stage of digestion emerge into consciousness any more than what we ingest physically does" is to describe a domestication of a wild beast.[2] Nietzsche's portrait is of distraction rather than wakefulness inasmuch as inner speech, as we saw, is prelude to a new level of awareness. That inner speech need be mollified, palliated, pacified, and muted signals a misconception of disruptor and disrupted alike. While it is true that unaware, inner speech goes on and on—testimony to its (and our) nonstop condition, nevertheless, when stopped, the awareness may face a choice implied by that knowledge. That choice is of movement and alteration.

When not subdued by an establishmentarian role, the anarchaic function breaks the hegemony of retention. Memory holds onto that which conceals the ungraspable point, the unmemorable, the amnesic, the blank. The blank is at every point that memory is—everywhere! It is a shadow cast by each word sound, an aura around each event, an atmosphere each thought breathes. It waits, perpetually ready to smother or engulf the material of memory and take things back to a pre-mnemonic condition. It is akin to an originary point (like Locke's state of nature or Hume's spirit of sympathy) in that we notice its displacements but not its action. It is like an invisible arche from which all genealogical lines emanate. It is the beginning of all subsequent beginnings. It predates, antedates, and postdates all beginnings.

The intial action of disruption opens awareness to inner speech—a kind of death of intellect, or its regeneration. The noise that is capable of engendering madness can more quickly close the ear of listening. Either course belongs to reaction, not intention. It is the direction of further action, absent in Nietzsche's account, that attracts me now. A greater disruptive force further eases the grip of conceptual order, provoking further reaction . . . or furtherance. Reaction is to a threat of exposure, furtherance, to a promise of freedom. As the hold disintegrates, another order emerges. To lessen the weight of intellect is to permit an equilibration with the weight of the soma, hitherto unsensed. The deeper action of an anarchaic function is to turn awareness beyond the arche of thought, its raw substance, its unprocessed *hyle*, its state of nature, its stuff.

If we return to Hume for a moment, an embryonic perception is present in the section "Of the Origin of Ideas." He tries to discern the difference I noted above, the divide between thought and impression. This much is clear: the productivity of thought is representation. A mirror is its model. It is a species of repetition. It duplicates, reduplicates, doubles, copies, fascimilates, utilizing methods of mass production, the assembly line. As to what is duplicated, the duplicandum itself, that is obscure. Hume admits that

> when we reflect on our past sentiments and affections, our thought is a faithful mirror and copies its objects truly, but the colors which it employs are faint and dull in comparison of those in which our original perceptions were clothed.[3]

The original of perception either lies near to thought or so much beyond that it is never revealed. It, the duplicandum, is near at hand if we take it to be clothing, covering, garmenting, attiring, embellishing, or protecting. Difference amounts to degree, shades of color, tones and hues—the rainbow again. It is the difference of equals, measurable increments, objectivity and safety. But what if that which is duplicated had no affinity to sympathy, resemblance, and likeness? Then, the naked and untampered perception that hides beneath the garb is infinitely beyond. Then difference itself is a veil unveiling. Then difference is the disruption engendered by hidden treasure, adding its immeasurable wealth—for better or worse—to the lot of perception.

There is, to be sure, a preliminary disrobing that is unavoidable. I refer to the unadorned "sensations or movements" that Hume attributes to a perceptual situation. Their presence in the presence of inner speaking follows the stop to another level. It is clear that Hume cannot follow. He is Moses glimpsing the promised land, forbidden to enter because of prior dealings with idolatry. His transgressions belong to those idols of the tribe, "human understanding [being] like a false mirror, receiving rays irregularly, distorts and discolors the nature of things by mingling its own nature with it."[4] Among the riches of his inheritance is the Enlightenment concept of sensation. As in Locke before him, a division is no division, but a sameness. Parsing ideas into reflection and sensation (as Locke does) appears to lend immediacy of somatic awareness to the second. They would then be part of a level in which unmodified configurations of energy shape a consciousness already fluent with reality, a consciousness offering minimal resistances to influxes from the world. This is not, however, the case. Ideas of either variety are "derived," much as metal is from ore by a suitable manufacturing process. Ideas of sensation are as much a product of intellect as are those of reflection. Only the apparent source is different:

> External objects furnish the mind with ideas of sensible qualities which are all those different perceptions they produce in us; and the mind furnishes the understanding with ideas of its own operations.[5]

Difference evaporates in the heated question of *how* objects "furnish the mind" with the matter of perception. That which lies anterior to objectification, that "something I know not what," is inaccessible to the perceiving mind. To ascribe responsibility to it for the production of ideas is to embrace an epistemology of distance where things magically cause perceptions. This ultimately yields an ethics of sorcery.

Between Locke's sensation and reflection lies no real difference because both are intellectual achievements, "having ideas and perception, being the same thing."[6] By the time "sensation" becomes sensation, the soma has been purged from the mixture.

Understanding has been innoculated against corporeal disruptors such as "itch," "pang," "tickle," "prickle," "twitch," and above all, "pain." A vaccine works by the law of similars so that a likeness—its semantic representation—is given for each disruptor, and becoming lodged in the mind, prevents the bodily event from breaking through. Immunized by sameness, object consciousness is unassaultable by difference through the soma. The world has been made free of disease!

As heir apparent to the elimination of corporeal disruptors, Hume faces a mighty dilemma. Either the source of sensation's greater vivacity is a mystery (it "arises in the soul originally, from unknown causes") or its study belongs to a field other than philosophy.[7] In a way, rather than find a passage between, he embraces both horns. The mysterious origin of sensation "belongs more to anatomists and natural philosophers than to moral," and shall be deferred to them.[8] Either case absents somatic interruption from the productive intellect. Dull commodities are preferable to a mysterious liveliness because their properties are measured, stable, and predictable. The other's force—that can white out dullness—is both superior and undesired. This epistemology of the second rate paves the way for a morality of the skeptic.

In reality, when Hume writes, there are two impressions, the entity itself and a vaporous double. Only here, red twin and white twin seem to have their identities confused. The impression, the "original sentiment" that is copied as an idea, is neither vibrant nor strong, but is touted as such, *is* such in relation to thought. Its mysterious translucent shadow that stalks the being of perception, threatening it with eclipse, appears nonexistent, insubstantial, unimportant to mention. Unproductive, its accomplishments are unrecorded. It doesn't even warrant a proper name. [What the deuce is her name? It almost came to me.] In absence, however, it wields a vibratory force sufficient to render any event exclamatory. Its "redness" lies in its greater proximity to the blood than the "original sentiment."

Through twinning, Hume's stride is not stopped by the dilemma. Nor is he is by the body of the impression—not the white cadaver consigned to anatomy classes but the red somatic form disowned by empiricism. The body is a phantom limb. The form is cognitively formless. Without qualities, modes, or attributes, it is not quite nothing. The act itself of twinning is an inspiration from the excommunicant, in its persistent affinity for things cognitive. What consciousness once had sympathy for and now rejects abounds in relation and likeness. Beyond the limits of reason, awash in the sea of similitude, resemblance takes a human form, the form of somatic awareness. That second, the subtle body, beckons to Hume even as he rushes to complete the walls of his mental compound. It summons, even through the processed stuff of objectified perception since its life is uneradicable.

PERCEPTION OF THE FORMLESS AND FORMLESS PERCEPTION

An escape clause, the twinning of impressions is at the same time a confrontation with a human percipience—or would be so were it not for Hume's intellectualist approach. The tentive focus of intellect establishes limits, boundaries, and confines within which to perceive form. A world of objects—rocks, trees, birds, stars, people—leaps up! Concerning the framing of focus, thought merely enumerates the conditions of all possible objectifying experience. Kant's transcendental methodology and its spawn continue to peer *through* the frame, which is to say, to gaze retentively. The view is toward how to perpetuate intellect, to own in perpetuity its endowments and property, to subject the state of nature to it. The exercise justifies itself by enshrining its results in a philosophical vocabulary of focus. By focus alone is intellectual sense retained. Only through intellectual meaning is focus imparted to experience.

The double I speak of is an unframed, nonfocal accompliment to a cognitively endowed impression. Its likeness derives from the matrix of similitudes to which it belongs, not from a representational duplication or duplicity. It therefore is empowered to shadow an object of perception the way the background shadows the thing in the foreground. Its shadowing is a thereness without a thatness—an unparticularisable universal. It is sensation, virginal with respect to the defilements of mind. It is a dimension higher than depth that at each point defines depth. It is the hidden body.

Hume's intellectualism requires the persistant deception of a Rebecca to confuse the twins. By sleight of hand (and a naive heart), he manages to accomplish just that. If "all impressions, that is, all sensations either outward or inward, are strong and vivid," force is a measure of an underived, nonparsitic, unruined condition.[9] Strength measures the degree to which the impression is steeped in the body milieu. The more fully *of* the soma, the more it is unavailable to the tentive character of mind. As a local movement of energy of somatic awareness, it is contained within a matrix of energy configurations defined by cross reference and self-enclosure. It is thereby related to corresponding movements, both local and global, that are currently energized. These part-part or part-whole relations shape the specificity of an impression as it gathers, crests, and falls off—or is renewed—before giving way to another movement. Like musical chords that blend, augment, give way, and diminish, local movements combine into a single moment of awareness, uniquely textured, animated, and colored. What reference they make is to similar currents of somatic awareness, or "kinaesthetic flows," as Husserl calls them.[10] The matrix of energy configurations is, therefore, a semiotically self-sufficient "system" of movements, postures, poses, gestures, and attitudes—a language. Although a matter internal to the matrix, meaning may be bled, with loss, in order to vitalize translation. Translation into object consciousness both weakens the concentration on soma and strengthens it on intellect: Rebecca's duplicity. It is upon this ploy that intellect seizes.

Freeze, frame, focus. The initial of definition is a border. Unless limited, it cannot be an impression *of* a something. It then remains an unproductive impression. It is slag, dross, cinder—the antiutilitarian. It is the ungodly, since God "has given the earth to the children of men" to make use of.[11] To gaze through the transparency of the frame is to perceive productively, to still the ceaseless movement of soma, to gather knowledge in the death of such movement. That eternal frozen moment, portrayed magnificently by Renaissance painters, stands as a monument to the divine. And the unsightly, vulgar, mundane worthlessness of a cognitively uninformed impression? It takes Kant to recognize its greatness. He notes "sensation is just that element which cannot be anticipated . . . and which therefore constitutes the distinctive difference between empirical and *a priori* knowledge."[12] An unanticipated shadowing, "sensation occupies only an instant [*Augenblick*]"—or less.[13] Opaque, untranslatable, irreducible, fluid, and unframed, sensation blurs intellectual focus—a catcall just when the mind is taking aim. Since objectified knowledge depends unconditionally on order and expectancy, sensation, the matter of perception, must be excluded.

To leave out the great and build on the less than great, the miniscule, trifling, and petty. Even Kant's penchant for consistency is strained to its rational limits by the contradiction that sensation—a primal disruptor—poses to his system. It *eo ipso* is the matter that makes the empirical experiential insofar as it interrupts the a priori productivity of intellect. Nonstop production halts in the face of the event. Superior in vital respects, it causes a momentary insurrection in consciousness. Anticipation lies in shambles. The hoped-for, desired, preplanned, programmed show is shunted to another channel while sensation floods the receptors. Experience thus announces itself. Yet this selfsame announcement must be squelched if the regularly scheduled broadcast is to go on. Kant acknowledges acute dismay:

> For it does indeed seem surprising that we should forestall experience precisely in that which concerns what is only to be obtained through it, namely, its matter. Yet nonetheless, such is actually the case.[14]

Reason triumphs over common sense as he swallows surprise rather than be swallowed by the bottomless maw of sensation.

Kant's vast intelligence is perplexed by another aspect of sensation. The unanticipated call of its opaque material exerts a gravitational force on objectifying consciousness, pulling it from schematization, and conceptual synthesis toward . . . a different sense. The different sense is a sense of difference: force of disruption. It breaks into indifferent categorial processing (quantity, quality, relation, or modality) with a manifesto: that *this* is real. The inexplicable sense of reality, an addition to perception, voices sensuous disruption. Conversely, reality provides a conduit for the matter of perception, sensation. Because sensation wells up with the blood of similitude, what we hear or see, taste or touch, is *like* the real. Kant searches for a place of reality within his system of thought. What he finds is unique: "what corresponds in empirical intuition to sensation is reality (*realitas phaenomenon*)."[15] Correspondent to sensation in an objectified manifold is, not form (since that is space and time, the form of all perception) or content (since that is without place) or both or neither. What corresponds is, surprisingly, that "the concept of which in itself points to being (in time.)"[16]

The unfocussed, unfrozen, unframed: the disruptive. Sensation, the red twin, the twin duped out of his human birthright, bursts through the foundation of intellectual knowledge. That which cannot be captive to categorial exploitation reappears, a beautiful or terrifying angel. Exclamatory, profane, declaiming, temporal being is unearthed. Existence, never a category or predicate, is back again. Unadorned sensation conveys or is conveyed through existential awareness.

Against an undifferentiated background—a blank—of somatic awareness, sensations are isolated, identified, and objectified. Predispositions for a vast perceptual apparatus are given by birthright, but their use must be imprinted by experience. ("No innate ideas!") On the tabula rasa of the soma, conceptually endowed percepts appear. They occupy the foreground because of their utility in thought constructions and in a manipulation of the world toward which intellect inclines. In a production-driven configuration, attention is primarily bound up in their identities. Preselected, prefigured, and preoccupied, it is unattuned to the solitications of the background. The ear for intellectual accomplishment is deaf to an appeal of existence ("being [in time]"). Though basis of all perception, a global awareness of soma is not taken in by the gaze. It is unperceived.

The gaze, eye of retentivity, takes the white twin in but not the other. The second is too swift, too kinetic for staring. Kant, in another spirit, says that percepts without concepts are blind. But this is to see invertedly since blindness is in the mind's eye with respect to conceptually unendowed perception. Perception ordinarily is blind to the red twin, herald of existence, because the gaze loses its way in being-in-time. Global somatic awareness is opaque. Its nontransparency means that "light" fails to penetrate. Since it operates by freeze frame, the *lumen naturale*, the natural light of understanding, of Descartes is unable to glimpse the soma. The lumen's power is broken up by the disruptive movement of somatic energies. Its vehicle, a lens fixed at a distant point in the interior darkness, cannot detect the kinesis of soma—soma itself.

Eyes open and light from afar pours effortlessly in. A world leaps up, caught by the same strobe! Fixed focus (minor adjustments aside) plus a distance point equals gaze without exertion.

DISRUPTION

The utter and complete transparency of the visual world that Kant labels an a priori form of intuition, a condition essential to any perception, is simply a glorification of the ease of vision. Space is visual, the space of geometry, first and foremost that through which light travels, and where impeded, discloses objects. Since transmission of light (of whatever variety) takes place on its own, Kant's is a bestowal of glory on perception purified of conscious trying. Transparency, a voiding of attentional effort and a surrender to automaticity, is a denial of disruption.

Space as utter transparency. Where light falls, it is one and the same space. Eyes open and sight leaps across the gap. What gap? There is only distance without difference, the distance of indifference. Transparency is utterly indifferent to itself. It costs nothing to give light passage. Thus, no difference erupts between eyes and world. They are of one space, one transparency—the *cogito*. The lumen naturale abolishes difference and establishes the reign of sameness, measured increment, degree, gradiant, rank, graded intensity. There is no opposite to the lumen, to space, to transparency, only that which is not yet seen, geometrized, and light bearing. The infinite optimism of Cartesian science derives from this abolition. Once difference is exiled, opposition becomes complementarity. "If not now known, it will be known." Progress is an inevitability.

When instrumented for production, perception maintains a passive oblivion of existence, save for a supervenient sense of reality, tamest of disruptors. At the same time, existential perception is a shadowing of cognitively endowed perception. Since it is a shadow of the higher, we can properly speak of it as a foreshadowing or prefiguring of the lower. From beyond retentive grasping, the first persists as that which elicits the second. Its emanation evokes the whirring mind to make sense of the event, and the rest goes from there. It embues cognitive processing, its mechanical synthesis of sense experience and concept, with ontic and ontological significance. It adds difference to the product of sameness. In hidden ways, it thereby distinguishes the actual from the possible, waking from sleep, truth from idle dreams.

It is, however, not correct that global somatic awareness eo ipso is awareness of existence. The global field, greater than the sum of local fields, arises progressively or all at once. Within somatic field, global or otherwise, currents of energy are joined with attention. In addition to intensity (Hume's force and vivacity), each has direction, duration, "thickness," clarity, and quality. One blends with, superimposes itself on, cuts off, fades into, or adds to other currents. The relatedness of one to another current, located in separate parts of the field, depends on a global presence. Without sufficient definition of the whole, sensation appears an episodic, intermittent, and singular event. Even when sensation begins to stand on its own, somatic processes in one locale appear unrelated to those in another.

The *progressus* toward a global presence, instantaneous or protracted, in itself does not approach existential awareness. Increasing degrees of integrity, release, and power signify a well-maintained global field but not the specific resonance of being-in-time. Existence arrives, if it arrives at all, as a disruption to a global sensation. It is not more of the same but a breakthrough from above. An unknown addition abruptly appears in relation to the global field. Existential awareness equals global somatic awareness plus *x*. *X* is a specific awareness of the arche name *I*. The articulation of existential awareness is *That I am*.

Unless the soma makes a difference, the arche name is not heard. The sound of *I* is not the pronomial token I, *je*, *ich*, . . . that designates a variety of persons. The relation between the token and the arche name must be uncovered since it does not exist at the level of public communication. It is not a token of exchange or multiplicity. The specificity of its resonance—*I*—breaks up the monotony of intellectual production and recalls me to the difference I make. Though the arche name is, therefore, a primary disruptor, the meaning of disruption is vacuous without a receptive somatic awareness. In different ways, Hume and Kant both illustrate this fact. Hume emphasizes the intermittancy of disruption to stage his denial of real identity, the *I*. He intellectually acknowledges a call and its discontinuity, but without a substantial, somatic basis to his philosophy, founders on the shores of negation. Kant, by contrast, stresses an absolute continuity of the *I*, but only as a necessary condition to intellectual productivity:

> It must be possible for the "I think" to accompany all my representations, for otherwise something would be represented in me which could not be thought at all, and that is equivalent to saying that the representation would be impossible, or at least would be nothing to me.[17]

DISRUPTION

This is no arche name but its semantic ghost. It is no actuality but a logical mode, namely that "insofar as I can grasp the manifold of the representations in one consciousness, do I call them one and all *mine*."[18] The *I* has become the reflex grip of retentivity itself. A device that protects itself from disruption.

Protects from what? From within the sameness of intellect, the soma appears. From within the sameness of soma, *I* appears. These are separate disruptions, different steps. They are ascendent. Vitality, quality, and inclusiveness increase, not by degrees, but by quanta. A human being opens to an actuality of impermanence, movement, and disruption.

TWO DIGRESSIONS

Nirvikalpanic and Visayagatic Perception in Advaita Vedanta

The specific difference I am urging between objectified and non-objectified impressions echoes one of Advaita Vedanta. In the Upanisads, it is said that

> *manas* is for men a means of bondage or liberation . . . of bondage if it clings to objects of perception (*visayasangi*) and of liberation if not directed toward these objects (*nirvisayam*).[19]

The first, or visayagatic, perception has already appropriated somatic events for knowledge production. Manas, intellect, has already made a subtle incursion into somatic energy configurations. As its retentive presence alters the somatic condition, it conceals the deed from itself. It explains the arising of impressions as *de novo*, or the metaphysically unknowable. Visayagatic perception conforms to the strong condition Locke establishes for the retentive character of mind: "whatever alternations are made in the body, if they reach not the mind; whatever impressions are made on the outward parts, if they are not taken notice of within, there is no perception."[20] It also takes the theme of a grammatical first-person subject, in the language of Vedanta, the *antahkarana*. The grammatical fragment or "I maker" bears no relation to the arche name *I*. Nonetheless, addition of "I" is an essential, *the* essential, phase of knowledge production. "I saw a bird," "I heard the wind," "I touch the tree."

Nirvikalpanic perception, the red twin cheated out of its birthright, is unsuited for intellectual productivity. Savage and natural, it has not been touched by a property-making mind. No invasive clinging, no manipulative appropriation on the part of manas has taken place. Its "indeterminateness" furnishes knowledge of pure existence (*sanmatra*). By contrast, an absence of personal appropriation, of "I making," marks the perceptual event. The absence is a disruptor that brings visayagatic perception to a stop. The *antahkarana* ceases to "go out" and hunt for somatic currents to appropriate. Quietened, the attention no longer disturbs a state of consciousness (*caitanya*) that is turned toward itself.

On Visual Geometry

We may think of perception in the image of the equipage. The object of perception is the horse, the driver—the mind—the carriage, the body, and that which would be the passenger, the *I*. Retentive grasp of the reins of perception then presupposes a fixed connection—the shaft—between objects and the body. It was not until discovery (or rediscovery) of the means of connection that the tentive character of mind came into full bloom. That which permits a human body to be related in a fixed, secure, and stable way to other bodies is a certain conception of space. Locke is among the first to notice that if the gaze is to illuminate bodies, it must be able to fill them with its luminous vision. Space, whatever its other properties, must be independent of objects. I quote Locke at length:

> For whether we consider in matter itself the distance of its coherent solid parts and call it in respect of those solid parts extention; or whether, considering it as lying between the extremities of any body in its several dimensions, we call it length, breadth, and thickness; or else, considering it as lying between any two bodies or positive beings, without any consideration whether there by any matter or not between, we call it distance—however named or considered, it is always the same uniform simple idea of space, taken from objects about which our senses have been conversant; whereof, having settled ideas in our minds, we can revive, repeat, and add them one to another as often as

> we will and consider the space or distance so imagined, either as filled with solid parts so that another body cannot come there without displacing and thrusting out the body that was there before; or else as void of solidity so that a body of equal dimensions to that empty or pure space may be placed in it, without the removing or expulsion of anything that was there.[21]

A container the gaze lovingly fills. But what if the gaze should lose itself among the objects it adores? The veil (*velo*), a second condition, was devised to this end by early Renaissance workers. The veil mediates between eye and object-laden space by interposing a grid. It disrupts with a patchwork of squares, each of which confines and protects the look from self-loss. Within each confine, sight is free to wander yet safe from overzealous adoration. The veil repeats a twin discovery of Euclid who found a parallel between optics and geometry. Virtually the same laws of one are found in the other, as a joint reading of his *Geometry* and *Optics* shows. Euclid begins by imagining every point in space as a potential eyepoint. Euclidean space is visual, or visual space is geometric—whichever way you want to say it. The veil, exemplar of both, reminds the gaze of spatial coordinates. Since coordinates (1,1) and (1,2) are adjacent, no gap between the two exists. The veil prevents a rupture of vision. Once accustomed to noting present location, the eye risks little by way of getting lost.

The infinite too can be geometrized. Take the point of vision as a center from which radii extend into a horizon of the plane of the canvas. Draw a midway line to intersect the radii, and from the point of intersection, connect with the central axis. Where all lines converge lies an infinity, the vanishing point. The vanishing point is the limit to which gaze can safely travel.

Brunchelleschi's rediscovery of the vanishing point of linear perspective is important because it confirms there is a geometric proof of a knowledge limit. This was the philosopher's stone of the Enlightenment, a thought bold and simple. Just as the eye encounters a point beyond which it cannot go, so to the mind's eye. To recognize the mental point is to be in a position to say what is and is not genuine knowledge—to have absolute control over the means of knowledge production. Linear perspective empowered thinkers to seek the corresponding point in intellectual space. Hume claims discovery in his derivation of ideas from impressions. He says,

> though our thought seems to possess this unbounded liberty, we shall find upon a nearer examination that it is really confined within very narrow limits, and that all this creative power of the mind amounts to no more than the faculty of compounding, transposing, augmenting, or diminishing the materials afforded us by the senses and experience.[22]

Kant makes a similar claim when he adapts a version of Hume's principle, and set the knowledge limit in the rules that govern the objectification process. Similarly, he argues: "We then assert that the conditions of the *possiblity of experience* in general are likewise conditions of the *possibility of the objects of experience*."[23]

Euclidean geometry begins with two extensive entities, point and plane, and derives the second from the first. The familiar conception of space results from an unequilibrated polarity of point and plane, when a single plane is fixed at infinity. The vanishing point of linear perspective represents this "absolute" plane. Fixity equals safety equals retentivity. But what if other geometries offered altered, risk-laden conceptions of space? Since the gaze's hegemony rests on the primacy of Euclid's geometry, another version is potentially destablizing.

I will below take to the case of projective geometry. Projective or synthetic geometry reverses the primacy of point and plane and maintains a dynamic polarity between the two. The resultant space will offer means of embodying the consequences of a disrupted intellect.

RECAPITULATION

Closely related to the Latin *sentire*, from which the words sense and sensation derive, is *sentis*, a path. It is that by which one feels one's way. Implied is a lack of foreordination. To feel from close up means to surrender an effortless, spatialized perception for discovery-in-immediacy. The faculty of foresight, foreknowledge, and foretelling lies in intellect. To control the means of producing experience, it attempts to subdue the impulse of pathfinding, the sentire. The soma, that through which wayfaring moves, is the *terra incognita*, barbaric, disruptive. Its emissaries—primary somatic movements—threaten to break the focus of intellect and unhinge information from the machinery of action. The stance of intellect therefore becomes retentive: to hold to its possessions and forestall all possible interruptions.

To maintain the position verges on contradiction. For within mind itself exists an anarchaic function. It both responds to disruptive forces arising from another level and initiates disruption. It instruments the stop. The stop neutralizes intellect's productive mechanism, resensitizing perception to the fruits of immediacy and to, as Kant says, being-in-time. It rectifies an imbalance inherent in conceptual analysis by opening the field of somatic consciousness. Human wholeness ceases to be an abstraction and becomes a way to embody.

The anarchaic function necessitates a reexamination of the modernist notion of perception. For one thing, the subtle intrusion of intellectual apprehension remains concealed with it. For another, in its assimilation of perception to judgment, it desensitizes the very milieu in which percipience transpires—the soma. Only an account compatible with the perceptual dynamics of the body itself—one that does not impose intellectual controls on production of raw material for knowledge—can provide a context in which disruption has meaning.

II

TRANSITION TO MOVEMENT

ARGUMENT

An anarchaic function ruptures the automaticity of mind. We experience the disruption of memory as we know it (Husserl's retentive and protentive activities) by wakeful consciousness—itself a remembering. When Husserl connects retention (and protention) with entropy, the *Herabsinken*, time becomes the maintainence of the same. Temporality must protect itself from the intruder: disruption. The self-protective stance (fear of discontinuity and nonexistence) expresses itself somatically as contraction. The contracted organic condition takes on a language of pathology, which in turn leads to a somatic critique of retention. The critique is useful in uncovering a suffering logos and transforming it to a logos of suffering. It also reveals the limited nature of a self-constituting consciousness. An alteration of consciousness, which is the possibility of an awareness that does not constitute itself, depends on opening toward the soma, in its "pure" or hyletic mode. Altered consciousness is the result of a given impulse or of a certain initiation. Awareness of the anarchaic memory provides a way of cultivating an initiative to relate to the other. An ethics that does not indulge in the fantasies of self-constitution lies in this direction.

There is disruption that is disruption by a memory. It interrupts what is past—a memory of how to reproduce the past—by remembering what is forgotten. What is forgotten takes precedence by being of the utmost importance. At the same time, what is forgotten is not that way by accident or happenstance, as in not being able to remember a friend's name. The forgotten wears the suit of accident while in its essence it is the immemorable, the amnestic. A memory of the essentially immemorable fades and cannot last though I may recall what occasions it. An attempt to hold on to it is defeated before beginning. It is the essential forgetting that disruption remembers. It is the rupture of the automatic by wakeful consciousness.

3

HUSSERL AND INTERNAL TIME CONSCIOUSNESS

In a bold stroke that took centuries of forebearance to overcome, Locke assimilates memory to sameness. The remembered is made continuous with the present since remembrance is a decay, a withering, a loss of freshness of the once present. Since devitalization takes place by degree—like a color fading in the course of time—the remembered past is a version of the present moment uninterruptedly and incrementally depleted of life. The present echoes on in memory, with sounds progressively weakening. Better still: we can follow the footfall of a declining impression, never once losing our way, until it blends in with the uniform blank of the unremembered. This is because memory involves mere deterioration of an impression, not distortion, transfiguration, or metamorphosis. Projected inwardly, the thought yields the conservation of the past. Projected objectively, Locke's thought becomes the uniformity of nature. Present resembles past, and future present, without sudden, unexpected shifts in law. Because sameness, modified by degree, extent, measure, or scope, regulates the movement of time; the unanticipated, Kant's description of sensation, is a factor included in neither memory nor nature.

Retention is the guarantor of diachronic sameness. It sets itself against difference. A reflex of self-will, it denies a place to disruptive chaos, thereby preserving the order of passing impressions. There will be no volcanism of events. Just as a mummified body still looks like a body, memory will transform nothing. An event that violates the rule of sameness is a nonevent, uncommemorated, cast out from the house of being. The exceptional-to-memory is unremembered.

In his extensive analysis of the intellectual production of sameness, Kant shows little concern for memory. Relegated to empirical psychology, "reproductive imagination" requires over one hundred years more to be granted analysis. Completing the work begun by Hobbes and Locke, Husserl, in *The Phenomenology of Internal Time-Consciousness* (1905), details how an impression lapses and in lapsing gives over to memory. So central is the devitalizing process that Husserl (following suggestions of Aristotle) designates it the "temporalization of human being." Inasmuch as the movement of time is defined by the fadeaway of life, temporalization is made the arch enemy of life processes, the emissary of death that is depicted in the hourglass run out.

Husserl's account bears a familiar stamp of the earlier work of British empiricism. An originary event (say, a musical tone) has a special brilliance that does not remain stationary; it belongs to the "running-off phenomena" [*Ablaufsphanomenene*]. Husserl's choice of terms suggests the gaze of an unmoved observer disturbed by the way things get away, elude the eye, escape, flee: "It would be better if they stayed put." The suggestion of perturbation is strengthened by the fact that the event's brilliance is susceptible to a sinking down [*Herabsinken*]. Debility, loss, weakening, withering, growing insipid are intrinsic to the character of Herabsinken. The more an observer watches, the less of an event there is to watch. To behold an event over time is to behold the remains of the event more and more—to witness a dying away. The role of observer is more tragic the more continuously it is occupied since it keeps watch over the decline of vital force. The gaze is a Sophoclean chorus, internalized and eternalized.

The two characteristics, running off and sinking down, constitute the two dimensions of time. Husserl offers the diagram in figure 2:

The segment OE is the time-line insofar as it is Ablaufsphanomen; it begins at O with now. The segment OE' measures the loss of life, the Herabsinken, while the angle EOE' is the angle of declination, the angle at which the sun of the event sets. The double tragedy of observation (loss of life, loss of light) is, Husserl notes, unremitting in the sense of being continuous. Continuity of both dimensions is Husserl's great discovery. "If we go along the concrete continuity [OE]," he explains,

> we advance in continuous modifications, and in this process the mode of running off is constantly modified,

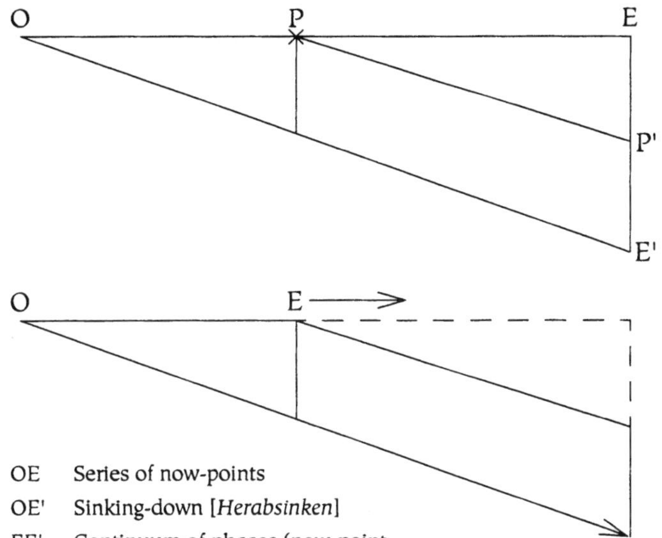

OE Series of now-points
OE' Sinking-down [*Herabsinken*]
EE' Continuum of phases (now-point with horizon of the past)
E→ Series of nows which possibly will be filled with other Objects

Figure 2

> that is, along the continuity of running off of the temporal points concerned.[1]

In fact, it is continuity itself that sinks down, weakens, drops toward zero, for "the entire continuity of the running off of the pasts of the preceding points moves uniformly 'downward' into the depths of the past."[2] Continuity, the crown jewel of temporal movement, that which ensures that the legacy of a past now is owned by a present now, is itself endangered by the merciless Herabsinken that pulls things toward remoteness, prehistory, the archaic. Continuity, which arranges just (read: predictable) inheritances from past to present, is not invincible. It too has an enemy. Oblivion, lethe, forgetfulness wait like a Saturn to devour the children of time, continuity included. And if forgotten, the unthinkable, immemorable: time would have a stop.

The tragedy of observation begins at O, the origin. Its foreknowledge concerns the destructive power of Herabsinken and the inevitable overcoming of time's redeemer, continuity. The savior has many guises and works miracles in many ways, for instance, in how the gaze retains an afterimage, as it were, of the event, of "impressional consciousness." Since for Husserl also, retention is prevention, a way to avert gazing at the inevitable, the escape he tries is through a new wrinkle: "when the tonal now, the primal impression, passes over into retention, this retention is itself again a now, an actual existent."[3]

Since the retentive strength of any single moment is doomed to fade, why not repeat the retentive grip on the faded, the withered, the already-passing-to-oblivion? To retain the retained multiplies the dissolving life of an impression, the way a hall of mirrors multiplies light. Multiples of retention can possibly forestall the inevitable. On the diagram, at a point of retention P that lies on OE, a wholly new continuity begins its sinking-down process, PP'. The invention can be repeated endlessly since "going along the flux or with it, we have a continuous series of retentions pertaining to the beginning point."[4]

The tragic gaze turns toward infinity to alleviate its suffering. The immemorial must not triumph over the infinite march of retentions. Will is thus turned toward refusal, the way a grip refuses loosening. Husserl's resort to a Zeno-like infinity to cross the gap of immemorability, however, yields Zeno-like paradoxes. Aristotle, above, alerts us to one primary one. We can differentiate phenomenologically between echo or afterimage and memory of an impression. The former is a reverberation that occupies a now and serves as origin for a continuity of retentions. The latter has no impressional content. Yet it can be a now that originates a wholly new retentional series, as in PP' of the diagram. Why then do we say that retention is of the past? Do we retain events in memory that never took place impressionally in the present?

In *De Memoria et Reminiscentia*, Aristotle asks: "why should the perception of the mere impression be memory of something else, instead of being related to this impression alone?"[5] His solution is to give retentional consciousness two handles. If gazed upon in itself, it is thought or presentation. If the gaze perceives it qua related to something else, it has the quality of likeness that characterizes fading away yet remaining similar to—retention. Aristotle's first option raises more questions than it puts to rest. If memory can be presentational, pared of its reduplicating function, then it must be differentiated from imagination, that is, "productive imagination." For Hume, this is possible because of a greater vivacity of the first, and the greater "liberty of the imagination to transpose and change its ideas."[6] This is a naivete, conjured by a gaze that believes itself omniscient. Memory is highly susceptible to influence and suggestion while imagination can be totalitarianistically imprisoned, giving it no play at all.

A similar naivete mars Husserl's account of the paradox of the retained retention. "The intuition of the past," he writes, "itself cannot be a symbolization [*Verbildlichung*]; it is an originary consciousness."[7] The thought is disingenuous because retention was invented to solve the problem of the past. Since presence is ungraspable, that which can be retained is the past as past. Its graspability identifies it as such. No further addition is necessary. "The contrast between the perception and the primary remembrance of an Object corresponds to that between 'now present' and 'past'."[8] The solution is voided if a special awareness is needed. Then, retention is a knob that opens no door. Its value become purely instrumental, to maintain a continuum as the essence of temporality.

Time for Husserl becomes maintenance of the same. Memory works heroically to avert the tragedy of becoming immemorial. In a Sophoclean way, remembrance pits itself against law and must lose. The whisper of an infinite resignation is the audible sigh of temporalization. "Every actual now of consciousness," Husserl writes, "is subject to the law of modification. The now changes continuously from retention to retention."[9] Even amnesia of the past, remote or near, does not alter the face of sameness. The not-retained, the lost to memory, the effaced, the repressed: these do not subtract any more than zero does. The law's magical action lies in its continuous operation, the continuity of continuity. Time is continuity continuously at work. Since any lapse in continuity is atemporal, the lapsing itself lies beyond the bounds of time. It is, therefore, immemorial, from the depths into which time sinks when it ceases to be human, when it becomes inhuman and devouring.

This is a remaking of time in a Protagorean vein. The law of modification projects an identical human consciousness, continuously remaking itself as one and the same, uninterrupted and uninterruptable by an altering force. The segment OE of the diagram schematizes the withering of self-identical consciousness whose stance precludes the exceptional. Frozen, hyperstructured, overorganized, it has lost a hunger for altereity. Spontaneity, the uncaused cause that can break the running off, the *Ablauf*, has been erased. Such exigence is for an unpremeditated, revolutionary shift in awareness—when the higher takes sudden precedence. All that lives in continuous time comes to a stop and one is face to face with the other-in-time, with other-time, with an altered temporalization.

This is the fractured line, shattered, violated, augured by a surd, a hole in the train of numbers. The nonevent deserves no mention in Husserl because from the far edge of the gap, continuity renews itself. Having been stopped, time begins again and in its retentional mode makes the broken segment whole. In memory, no record of the untranscribable exists: the break, the nullity, the difference. Time repeats the same story without end.

It is a story of self-calming. Object consciousness masters itself by dulling its fears—and thereby makes itself what it is. The story is one of consciousness repeating to itself, "I am not afraid," and thereby becoming what it is. That the story lacks an end shows the nature of the fear. Consciousness is in the mode of running off [Ablauf] because of its fear of facing the end of its time. The end of its time, the upsurge of the unretainable, the irrational, the unconditional—the other-in-time.

To overthrow the law of modification requires immoderation. But excess can begin modestly. An intersession keeps its force of interceding regardless of its scope, insurrectional or a subtlely obtrusive of difference. Repetition of the self-calming formula that constitutes consciousness is needed because of frequent rupture in the time line. The call of unretentionality is a commonplace, almost as common as its refusal. One need look only so far as the daily round.

4

TOWARD A SOMATIC CRITIQUE OF RETENTIVITY

A dislocating force that exerts itself in the midst of the mundane: does it originate from above or below? [Her name again? I remember she was from Omaha, but her name?] Marcel calls attention to the stop in the stream of automaticity. The resurgent factor has lability for its location. Marcel gives this description:

> I put my hand, let us say, into my pocket to take my watch out. I discover that my watch is not there; but it ought to be there; normally my watch *is* in my pocket. I experience a slight shock. There has been a small break in the chain of my everyday habits. . . . The break is felt as something out of the way; it arrests my attention, to a greater or a less degree.[1]

A threefold character of the event can be made out. There is an experience of being disrupted, "a slight shock," "a small break," a discovery of something missing. There is the disrupted: a routine check of the time, a habitual and automatic movement, meaningless in itself, a state of preoccupation. And there is the disruptor, clothed as arrest, "felt as something out of the way," a jolt of force that reveals the moment without giving itself away—a nontransparent event.

In the example, disruption occasions reflection, a reflective exercise that unrolls the day in order to account for the lost pocket watch. Object consciousness, with its predilation for problem solving, is alerted by the onset and takes off in high gear. It recalls the last time the watch was there, the circumstances, what happened next, and so on. Althought the disruptor itself is an unappreciated exception except insofar as it instruments intellectual scrutiny, Marcel's result is unexpected. The stop has become promptor for the very operation it arrests: consciousness's production of its self-productive conditions.

The oddness is in how submergence leads to more submergence, in the endless, moment-to-moment production of consciousness. Shadowings of somatic currents passing into impressions that yield a stable continuity of self absorb attention with no remainder. Self-absorption leading automatically to more of the same. Then abruptly, the stop! Under the guise of a missing object, the stop reclaims the attention from retention, identification, automatism. The exception to the law of modification enters the scene, thunderously, subtly. The precedence of the higher momentarily clears the stage. An awareness other than that of self-production charges the play with stillness. Recollection is recollected. The call to live up to an ethical potential, to be measured by an incommensurable quality, resounds.

Yet, after a sudden recollective burst, Marcel's focus veers back from the anarchaic to the productive function. What is the net result of disruption? Distraction interrupted, its energy drain stoppered, thought is redirected along a time line. It runs off. "Reflection has carried out its task and the problem is solved."[2] Disruption is harnessed to refocus intellect. Marcel's advance is no advance at all. His is an economy geared like the liberal democrats', Locke's and Kant's. The utility of disruption is no disutility, an interference with the flow of consciousness. It is a positive utility. Like a mighty river falling onto the blades of a turbine, it can be used to turn the wheels of thought. Technology intervenes to save civil order from disruption, and more! To render disruption continuous with civil society. Since technology is self-interested, once the intervention is carried out, it erases the disclosure of disruptive force itself.

Partial disavowal of disruption leads to obscurity. Marcel's motives grow obscure when the context is personal discovery. A similar economy appears to be at work. In the midst of being judgmental, "a memory comes back to me," he writes, and with the memory, a question of self-examination: "Was this act of mine really so very different from the act which today I feel inclined to judge so severely?"[3] The disruptor, a memory, emits an energy that illuminates hidden motives. Reflection follows. The questioning, guided by the force of light, gazes empowered by a sudden increase in luminescence. The movement, Marcel would want to say, is recollective in character. Yet it omits taking account of the nontransparent datum, the disruptor itself. To the extent it replaces one face to face with the enigma of the other, it echoes the call of the higher. In between, what we have is disruption carrrying out its indenture to objectifying consciousness. The stop disguised as "a memory" restarts the play of an awareness that calms itself in front of the abyss. Marcel can proclaim, "I have a certain sense of being set free . . . ; it is as if I had overturned some obstruction in my way." This mystifying freedom is bought with a heavy burden. In the coin of intellect, its cost prevents a greater liberation. The unimpeded replaces a freedom from self, from self-making consciousness, from a play that loses and recovers itself in front of a feared disruption. An epiphany is won, but at the expense of a potentially terrifying advent: a consciousness radically altered by the impress of the higher.

Continuous pull of retentivity. Can it be thrust aside long enough to bear its own critique? Blankness. Whatsitsname.

I have practiced one kind of critique, reminding myself how costly the economics of retention are. Locke's observation that "our thoughts, reasonings, and knowledge, could not proceed beyond present objects, were it not for the assistance of our memories" prompts a continuous monitor of the retentive capabilities. Consciousness obsessed with the thought that disorientation, delusion, imbecility, and insanity lie in ambush in an unmediated present is increasingly confined to the safe enclave of the past. The wolf-boy image symbolizes the feared deformation: a child reared in the wild, beastial, lacking language, memory, and other cognitive abilities, nonhuman. Vigilance, self-arming, a state of war, "of every man against every man," drains vital energy from impressional awareness.[4] The entire receptive sensitivity is reduced.

This is not all. An effective monitor requires a further line of defense. The gaze must be continuously on the soma. Vigilance toward soma wears the aspect of a frontier guard at the steppes. Looking both ways, toward civil and barbaric, the gaze constricts communication of meanings from one side to the other—in which somatic shadowing can inform and be informed by perception. Upon deleting memory of exchange and reciprocity, the attention is bound up in surveillance. A contracted condition has consequences for the life body. Retention gives over to tension. Tension constricts a circulation of energy that deforms the whole. The result is pathology.

Pathology is the continuous termination of disruption. Consciousness's obsessive fear of immediacy has left the gaze wary to the unanticipated. Wariness translates into a practiced desensitization that leads to atrophy. Evocations that once were refused no longer evoke response. Disruption is sublimated into fantasy whose phantasms further intensify the guarded state. Affectivity is modulated. Because affective response can release unpredictably large quantities of energy, opening onto sensate immediacy, extremities need to be avoided. Cathartic excess is precluded from expression. But it is not only a question of immoderation. Stress is placed on reactive feeling because it supports consciousness's obsession. Reactive feeling dramatizes a pathological avoidance of disruptive force. It continually acts out that which it fears meeting—discontinuity. In addition, an entire region of feeling life ceases to be inhabited. Nonreactive, positive feeling that empowers a receptivity to difference, disruption, and the intercession of the higher is fictionalized, trivialized, marginalized. The signification of key feeling terms is rendered vacuous by ambiguity.

Pathology is a three-fold deformation. I have just said how the *paschein*, the feeling element, is directed to serve retentivity by fostering emotions of closure. Sympathy, the feeling of *withness*, is eradicated, with devastating effects for the intellect. No free interchange is possible of sympathies, similitudes, affinities, resemblances, or affinities between soma and mind. The gates have been closed. An incomparably rich influx of percipience, rife with information about the world, is therewith sacrificed. Inasmuch as it relates to the place of consciousness in an open region of exchange—an ecology—there can be no substitute for it. Its knowledge of dependencies, conditions, influences, and permeabilities is not replaceable. As a result, consciousness begins its tale of autonomy, self-sufficiency, and sui generis—the completion of its Protagorean mission. It will meet its fear of disruption with self-calming and reassure itself that loss and recovery constitute the totality of subjectivity. It will grow analytical, critical, and pedogogical.

Least defended, the life body is most pathologically affected by the withering gaze of retentivity. With a circulation of inner sensation impeded, a renewing force no longer reaches all somatic regions. An equilibrium between metabolism and catabolism becomes destabilized, leaving the soma vulnerable to internal attack. While vital force makes a circuit, vulnerability is held in check and the life body rendered immune to disease. Fracture of the circuit and constriction of vital force decreases flexibility and resilence. Response to change is less informed by the body's contact with what is alien to its balance. Inappropriate or weakened response further disequilibrates the soma.

Disease—pathology of soma—is primarily a lack of freedom of responsiveness to disruption. Rigidification occurs before the onset of symptoms that are termed medical and are subject to treatment. As soon as a region is no longer rejuvenated, a dampening of its response to imbalance occurs. Under this condition, the attempt to regain balance will be frustrated by the lack of circulation. Frustration leads to displaced action. Symptomology is a language of displacement. A symptom is the displaced effort of the body to ameliorate a constricted circulation of vitality. Pathology thus presents an image of displacement, a record of deformation.

Pathological disease can be cured to the extent that a circulation of somatic energy can be reestablished. If rigidification has had irreversible effects on soma, disease is incurable. Cure involves restimulation of vital force and should not be confused with relief of symptoms. Cure requires a correct and careful hermeneutics. The text of symptomology must be carefully read and interpreted before prescribing that which will help reestablish balance. Lacking the hermeneutics, symptoms may be palliated by forms of treatment without affecting the basic course of pathology. Palliation has the effect of erasing the symptomological text, thereby executing further displacement, further contraction. The continuous termination of disruption follows a downward spiral of responsiveness to life, with increasing deadening of areas of consciousness. This is a way of speaking of death by death.

Pathology is nonetheless retentivity's way of meeting being. The pathos of paschein is sorrow, the passion. The ontology of object consciousness is suffering, partner to its ethics of separation. Since suffering need not be a negative that is a minus, it need not fuel the story of self-calming. Ontologically, as a privation to consciousness in its self-making, it brings a great measure of hope to consciousness, perhaps the greatest. Since physical suffering, pain of disease, is retention's own ontological possibility, to meet pain as such reopens the door to disruptive force. To cease running off in time and to feel *with* (sym-pathy) the suffering is to encounter the transformative power of disease. It is to remember, in a place of oppression, what takes precedence—an act commemorating the higher and its supervenient imperative in human life.

The shift from a suffering logos to a logos of suffering corresponds to that from hopelessness to hope, from paralysis to participation. Deficient knowledge is not so much made efficient as it is radically supplanted. A logos of suffering strives for acceptance and recognition. It does not alter the quality or quantity of suffering yet will accept alteration. Both a hermeneutics of disease and of suffering move independently of each other on different levels. I can face my lack of ease at the same time I seek to decipher the image of my symptoms. Their differences in power and scope correspond to the different pathologies of soma and feeling. To restore the body to health is one thing. To open feeling to the higher and to let it *feel* higher is another.

5

THE BETWEENNESS OF THE SOMATIC FIELD

The tentive character of mind—retentivity—reveals itself in the stop. The story of its obsession, with its allegory of separation, likewise stands revealed. Though monumental events, these discoveries do not nearly exhaust the wealth of the stop. They proclaim a self-constituting process of consciousness which, when heard, grows less obstreperous in the face of the neglected other. The emergence of somatic awareness, sudden or graded, is an initial phases of disruption. Even when elided into latter phases, its presence—the presence of the body, organic and corporeal—is the *conditio sine qua non* of cessation. The time-making mechanism, Husserl's running off, through which consciousness strives for a continuous grasp on its own character must cease momentarily in order for its negation to be sensed. When time has a stop, what is different surfaces to disconfirm consciousness's belief in isolation and solitariness. In the stop, somatic awareness emerges in alliance with intellect.

The emergence of the other moderates consciousness's demand for transparency—the gaze. Its fear of not being able to look, blindness, in ceasing to be paralytic, designates an approach to being. This blinded percipience, this nonlook, takes impressions *in* rather than capturing them in the net of cognitive analysis. The soma cannot be seen, reflects no light, and is a nonentity in the realm of the visible. That it fails to register in the visual spectrum gives it an other-worldly aura, the way immediacy appears to abstraction. Percipience cultivates a certain potency of the opaque, unsightly materiality of the body. It requires that the storytelling character of consciousness—how it needs to retain itself in order not to lose itself—subside and not project itself forward, protentively. Where difference is most piqued lies exactly in the matter of cultivation since to cultivate is to exert extensively and intensively for a specific project. Percipience is constituted by repetition of effort, coming back again and again. Sight is a reflex of the gaze which requires nothing in addition to a long-standing habit of turning to face and stare.

Percipience is already an altered consciousness. Consciousness no longer consumed by self-producing is expanded by a measure of courage. Hyperactive, overstressed objectification ceases to usurp the totality of resources and create an economics of scarcity. Objectification instead takes its place and remembers its function. Its forgotten destiny has to do with record and transciption—both retentive activities—in the face of repeated disruptedness. Across the gap, it carries a spark of initiation that kindles the fire of memory, remembering the immemorial. If not the only spark, it is the primary one for a human being that lives in recorded history, that speaks in conversation of history. For others of different traditions, other primary modes exist which also exist for us in nonprimary ways. For consciousness to recognize itself as spark is already an alteration since such recognition passes beyond self-recognition, toward what takes precedence in thought. This is an echo of Eckhart's thought:

The mind encloses something within itself, a spark of the intellectual power which is never quenched. This spark is the higher part of the spirit; in it is located the image of the mind. Yet in our minds there is also a knowledge directed towards external things, namely the knowledge through the senses and through reason. This knowledge proceeds by representation of images and by concepts, and it conceals from us that other way of knowing.[1]

Memory of the past, augury of the present: retention and protention transfigured. The self-containment of retentivity and the self-remembering of initiation: the Janus face stands on the doorpost of somatic awareness. With the economics of scarcity "rationalized," and the outposts on the steppes abandoned, free exchange is rediscovered. Not a conceptual demarcation of convenience and repression, the frontier between body and mind is exposed and permeable. It persists, independent of both, the recurrence of difference, the initial onset of the other. Hence, the opening phase of initation is felt as a "crossing the line." A traversal, complete with leavetaking and welcome, is the real gift of disruption, the token magically left in place of a force that eludes all memory. What is crossed is less a line and more a vacancy. The empty space between object and soma, the space that recurrently empties itself of grasp and gaze, is empty enough to contain both. Object shrinks to a specific locale, as if a perspective opened up the globe, while soma divulges its secret of tangibility. Soma is not yet the ground of consciousness but that in whose soil ground will appear. It is, however, earth to objectification whose "heaven" is filled with abstracts, conceptual prototypes, and ideals. This is Locke's heaven, whose archangel is Induction.

Given its fundamental perceptive nature, somatic awareness is allied to kinaesthesis (Husserl), coenesthesis (Marcel), or proprioception, but percipience is a nearer relation. To speak of *Abschattung*, a foreshadowing or adumbration of an object, is to cast a *look* at somatic awareness, to look askance, to have an ulterior motive. This is the case with Husserl's approach.[2] The "fore"-ness, the apriority, of shadowing can have its source only in object consciousness as it strives mightily to anticipate the unanticipated. The look is reticence, in reserve, but nevertheless, the fable of red twin/white twin is reenacted and the birthright again stolen. It is not the natural attitude, the gaze unabashed and forward, meaning, for Husserl, enforced, imposed, guarded, at war, martial, rigid. The sideways look or half look means evasive, camoflaged, decoy, cunning, disingenuous. He acknowledges that the second, looking without looking, is the more tenacious:

> The sensory fields appear only when we stop short of the motivated apprehension of the corresponding objective "sensory" aspect and this stopping short is difficult.[3]

Kinaesthesis is itself an accompaniment to a hyletic flow, the general circulation of energy throughout the soma. The place where one verges on the other has to do with where an identity emerges from a background that conditions a uniform percipience. Roughly, kinaesthesia is a term that suggests a somatic sense of motion, though in fact the life body is never without minute movements such as respiration, peristalsis, or circulation of the blood and lymph, The tenacity of a subtle, vaporous retentive attitude toward somatic awareness is felt when Husserl scrutinizes the hyle and concludes that

> to the constitution of the enduring object there is necessary a peculiarly psychic moment which takes the hyletic flow as the *Abschattung* of an enduring being, the apparent aspect.[4]

The hyle is merely *materia prima*, bare stuff, that which is beneath (sub-stance), unworthy of notice, dismissable. ("Hence it were better to avoid speaking of the hyletic field.")[5] The moment to speak of is that of grasping. The hyle's impenetrability is to penetration from outside, a violation by light. From a warm, vibrant internal pressure—a subtle body's presence—it offers no real resistance. Facing outside, it is guarded as it meets the guard's stare. Then it is the faceless other, the alien, the potential guerilla. Facing inside, it has readied the place for an unknown visitor, that one whose arrival will disrupt the usual course of events with unknown feeling. In actual fact, disruption consists in the shift from empty to full, zero to unity, and anxiety to composure. It is a reaffirmation of opacity and the fertile hyletic folds that, beyond knowledge, keep the treasure safely hidden until the moment of discovery.

Impenetrability and interpenetrability: I will (by my will) perceive and I let be perceived. The opaque barrier lies just beyond the farthest point from which light is reflected backward, like looking from inside the windshield of a car with the cabin light on at night. The opacity measures the tensile strength of the backward bent will. Where it is maximal, the dark is greatest. This seems the point of Marcel's enigmatic query, "up to what point is this interior opacity a result; is it not very largely the consequences of an act? and is not this act simply sin?"[6] Yet the creation of transparency—the gaze of retention—is no simple act that determines a fall or flaw subsequent to it. The light of intellect, the lumen naturale, is a creation so against nature that it must be enacted moment after moment. That consciousness by habit lights up the stage on which it plays out its story does not argue against continuous reenactment. It merely assigns responsibility to another dimension of will. Beyond the proscenium, beyond the most penetrating glance from the actors' eyes, the invisible barrier is really the farthest reach of solar radiance powered by the will's continuous fusion—its self-making. Within its magic circle, within its solitude, one is protected from interruption because slips, pratfalls, miscues, goofs, and out-and-out mistakes can be woven into the fabric of performance. Descartes's dictum that error concerns the will's overreaching itself is both absolutely right and absolutely wrong. Error is a misplay of the gaze but since its luminescence provides an infallibility, to misplay is still to take part in the story.

The dimming of the lights—search light, spot light, stage light—and the soma breathes a sigh of relief. An outpost designed for accusation and provocation is closed; the play is on intermission. The trope of night reasserts itself in metaphors of containment, proximity, and subsidence. A circulation of energy that moved in stealth, through constricted passages, neglectful of the far reaches, again has full sweep. The consciousness that rejoins this movement can bring none of the equipment of self-will. Off to a corner and subjected less to extinction than quarantine, objectification is less obtrusive and therefore less itself. Stripped of light, consciousness is often portrayed in figures of sacrifice, renunciation, repudiation, and self-denial. That is, it portrays itself as relinquishing a power voluntarily, in atonement for. . . . The fact is that the turn from the look and the turn from self-pity are one and the same, and that as long as the act of negation looks for approval, it is inauthentic. Consciousness is not altered by loss (since it has defined itself privatively) but by gain—a quickening. Disrupted, reminded of its affinity to the soma, consciousness *moves*, develops tempo, sets a rhythm, follows a cadence—it rediscovers difference.

Difference, the shift between motion and rest, is at the root of Aristotle's question that begins Book VIII of the *Physics*: "Was there ever a becoming of motion before which it had no being and is it perishing again so as to leave nothing in motion?"[7] Difference is no surveyer's boundary line between adjacent fields but an expunging of a frontier. The grasp on self-identity that seals the border yields an analysis of movement that separates it from the rest by equality, degree, and order. Since consciousness repeats the image of itself endlessly, privation offers an ultimate explanation: rest is deprived motion. Consciousness, starved, indigent, deprived, a tale that begins with a lack striving to recover itself then conceptually projects its play. The concept is congruent with and legitimated by a suppression and eventual stagnation of hyletic flow. The breakthrough of boundaries brings a release of what is pent up, the waters of life flow. Release to movement is a tangible result. Though it is felt while breakthrough—the disruptor—is not, we must not confuse Aristotle's question by assuming a gradual transition from rest to movement and back, of the kind the eye can follow. Freedom and release clothe the body of disruption the way a dress does the skin. They are at once veil and unveiling; they manifest a presence while hiding it from view. They are the vestige. The memory of what takes precedence, being ungraspable, leaves a palpable something as signature of its action.

To invoke the maternal in the question of movement by speaking of a quickening of consciousness is appropriate. Though the rest state of intellect is not repose but refusal of unrest, quietism is no solution to obsession unless hyperactivity is. Even then, since one's action springs from a reactive attitude, it serves only to perpetuate a negation of being. Action is never here, never now, but protentively directed. So-called movement of the body, the will's placing the body at its disposal, carries out conscious intention but only by enforced placement (a displacement) of limbs, presumption of postures, grasping by digits. The physical embodiment of retentivity is visibly stiff, directive, and managed in a manner that contrasts with a fluidity of motion that occurs once object conscious has accepted its place in the ratio. Proportionality and balance speak through the "gross movement of parts" if somatic awareness is allowed speech. The coming to articulation is a birth of sorts, a moving into movement after movement has been deadened. A resurrection of the life body, movement of this improvisational, respirational kind expresses a will-less nurturing of the soma's need to be. The approach is maternal in the way that ontological expression is, pregnant with the emergent that will rupture the present.

As long as consciousness is unable to recognize an opposition between rest and motion, it settles for the refraction of rest into unrest and back again. The schema for its internal dialectic, the problem propels consciousness beyond the present into a hypertemporality in which to figure out a solution. Problem, resolution, new problem: restlessness (striving to avoid the pangs of obsession) forces action to burst forth prematurely, rips it from a matrix of motivation like a young Caesar. Or, what amounts to the same, unrest stimulates the tentive character of mind, increasing the productive imagination's productivity. Like a Hamlet, consciousness is engaged in endless deductions following endless possibilities that it dreams up. Coordinately, the body is instrumented to carry out an intention without its own "will" having been consulted. As long as subjectivity is defined solely in terms of consciousness, the body is subjected to the rule of restlessness, an invitation to pathology. Unlike intellect, the body is not at its own disposal and cannot swell itself with self-constitution. If subjugated by a dismissive attitude, the body shrinks in its own skin, its expression growing more warped, muted, outside.

By bringing an opposition of rest and motion to movement, disruption offsets the frozen pairing of rest and unrest. A consciousness altered by movement is primarily altered internally, by the interior logos of the soma, circulation, recurrence, return. Any other so-called change of consciousness is imposed or imposter. Since it cannot be retained, an alteration by movement does not persist—any more than disruption can—since its temporality is of difference, not sameness. As retentivity alternates with irretentivity, the work of the somatic logos can be felt as an opening to sensitivity. Quickened and in tempo, a moving consciousness is not deaf to the vibratory specifics of the soma nor dumb to their meanings. Its praxis of moving *in* the somatic milieu is an acquisition repeatedly on the verge of being lost, yet it is by this balance *on the edge* that it brings itself to sensation. Bald, raw, undoctored sensation yields itself only to a proximate companion. Distance brings disguise and deception, the white twin. To be near is to be in movement, or else the life body rapidly recedes, like an artery under the thumb. In closeness, there is percipience and percipience is an attainment of the logos of the soma.

The paradox is that disruption—the breaking force—creates contact. Cutting through the continuous running off of phenomena, disruption momentarily ends the ethics of separateness. "Atoms of experience," in various states of devitalization are assembled to form molecular chains suitable for cognitive completion. Hume's observation that particles "bound together by some universal principle which had an equal influence on all mankind" uncovers consciousness's need for a logic of equality.[8] Universality, fraternity, and equality constitute democratic ideals once vitality must be parcelled out. Connection and distribution of goods (energies, revitalizations), moreover, can only be achieved equitably through mechanical means or else individual biases of color, taste, preference, like, and desire make for inequality. Hume finds association to be the model principle. Within the mechanism of association, we find a shadowing [Ablauf] of contact in the principle of contiguity, really the idea of adjacency or juxtaposition. ("The mention of one apartment in a building naturally introduces an inquiry or discourse concerning the others.")[9] Continuity in space and time "connects" through the distance of separate equalities, atoms that repel other atoms except when influenced by association. By means of a cessation of influence, atoms "disconnect," and a memory whose forgetting has been forgotten and whose remembering takes precedence over all pretense toward equity.

Altered by movement, a consciousness of contact knows contact not as a content or an intention but an eruption of being. As the attention "touches" the soma, an exchange, basis of all contact, occurs during which the soma "is touched" by the attention. The joining of two inequalities by virtue of felt exchange forms the model for all subsequent moments of face to face. Movement alters consciousness by conjunction, where the logos of the life body, not intellect, determines the dynamic. Conjunction is not an atemporal or omnitemporal event, nor less one that runs off endlessly saying "and then, and then." Furthermore, the ampersand, indicative of exchange, does not point to a process of becoming equal, as if two unequal basins of water were joined by a tube so that their levels equilibrated. The result of contact is that inequality remains unequal, but not the same. Remaining unequals, having become different, the conjuncts are each transformed.

Altered consciousness, consciousness in movement, is transformative consciousness. Since the initial and initiatory contact is with the soma, the life body is that to which consciousness is initiate. Intellectual logic must study at the knees of the logos of the soma if an appropriate response to the higher is sought. Since the unanticipated is sought, there is no logic primer, which does not at all mean that there is no teaching. The meaning of Marcel's remark that incarnation, the central "'given' is opaque to itself" is that somatic logic cannot be put into discursive or symbolic formulae.[10] The restriction applies to transcendental as well as empirical logic, to the categories of intellectual productivity as well as to "rules of reason." Though somatic logic is demonstrable, its demonstration is performative, interiorly or expressively (as in dance.) The effort to grasp the logos retentively is self-frustrating in that the result is the for-itself's transcription of its own transparency. Inasmuch as the transcript contains material that is paradoxical and counterintuitive, it critiques the limits that retentivity imposes on conscious activity. The willingness of consciousness to forsake the tenets of logic, to be alogical, is a precursor to contact. Seeking the space between two thoughts, consciousness is well prepared for the advent of a memory that remembers the immemorial, the anarchaic, the different.

Within the dynamic circuit of the soma, consciousness is less for-itself—repeating the story of its fear in order to disarm its fear—and more in-itself—not having chosen what is proper to and property of oneself. The moving or flowing consciousness is interspersed with the "I can," subjective impulses to accomplishment, which is associated to kinaesthesis proper. Husserl is clear on the relation: "The 'I can' works directly on or with kinaesthesis, and brings about sensational and hence objective changes only indirectly."[11] Though the striving to accomplish can arise from retentivity or irretentivity alike, the impulse shapes the soma. The gathering of somatic energy, concentration or alertness, is a memory of how to move into action: this limb raised and extended, that loosened, torso torqued, head down, and so on. Kinaesthesis as an embodiment of memory operates under a different imperative, as does the "I can," depending on whether mind or soma initiates the action. Subjected to retentivity, kinaesthesis tends to be deformed like an instrument under too heavy a grip. Within the hyletic flow, it has the potential of giving free, nonegoic expression to intention. That the "I can" can be potentized without engaging the objectifying apparatus results from contact, soma's interior contact with that which is higher and reminds one of the height. This "upper-level" connection is overlooked by Marcel, who claims action "is impossible unless I can identify and define objects."[12] The neglect advocates a quietism since doing itself is tainted by the obsessive fear of disruption. Once subjectivity is enlarged beyond the for-itself, an altered consciousness enables somatic memory of kinaesthesis to take precedent. I can, I am, are not separate vehicles of expression.

Whether interspersed with kinaesthesis or not, the somatic circulation possesses by virtue of contact the character of percipience. A dynamic of exchange that lets consciousness be agile, stopping the obsessive repetition of play and storytelling, also allows it to be touched by the world. Such touch is not a going outside itself, projective exteriorization, the running off of the for-itself, which then requires a catching up, an introjection, a coming back to the play. In perception, somatic awareness remains *with* itself, *in* itself, performing no maneuvers that counteract welcoming an impression. Its circulation is a current that magnetically attracts data to it, though these data are not retentionally and protentionally reproducible. They are, so to speak, fleeting anomolies in the hyletic flow, disruptive qualities that prick sensitivity, minute shifts that indicate the work of otherness. Perception animates consciousness, as Hume notes lamentingly, by being touched by animating energies arising on all levels. Our ordinary speech about perceptiveness is mindful of the brevity of its moment, the lightning flash of contact. An accumulated charge leaps across opposing poles, illuminating what the intervening space contains.

If not through reflection and transparency, how does altered consciousness perceive? Exchange, the joining of inequalities through contact, implies that the perceiving (*percipio*) and the being perceived (*percipi*) interpenetrate and are one with and in the perceiver (percipient.) The mutual offering, moreover, is possible only as long as contact remains since it is the third force, the *coincidentia oppositorum*, that frees movement and allows passage back and forth across a barrier. Since their different individualities remain, what is perceived does not become *like* the perceiving, or vice versa. Exchange is both a handing over and a taking back. For each participant, it is a subtraction plus an addition, a vacating plus an accumulating, an honoring plus a being honored, a sacrifice plus a triumph. In the reciprocity of taking from and giving over to, there is an intimacy of knowing that defies all difference—in type, scale, or level—because it precisely is a knowing of difference. In that moment, mortality can don the cloak of immortality, and imperfection that of perfection, and what then? Or as Yeats asks of Leda, with reference to the swan, "Did she put on his knowledge with his power?" Inasmuch as difference, the disruptive force, travels an anarchaic road, it honors no frontiers, pays no tributes to gatekeepers, and upsets the order of every camp it visits. Holding no thing, it passes through everything knowingly. To the extent that perception is able to partake of its passage—the exchange—its knowledge is comparable.

Because opacity is the limit of the logic of sameness—since beyond transparency of knowledge, only black fires of barbary burn—temporality is likewise altered. In contact, the running off and sinking down *(Hinabsinken)* of time that bought sameness with the coin of retention comes to a stop. Duration, permanence, self-identity: these ideas are part of the same transaction. Holding on to the machinery of production, consciousness while playing a managerial role, carries an obsessive and tragic fear of stoppage. It will be an abyssmal end to light, space, time, knowledge, doubt, recovery from doubt, the world, God. Time no longer retained in the interest of telling the for-itself's story is sudden, expansive, and explosive. Its perceptive power is capable of conveying energies of which ordinary temporality contains only a trace and whose retranscription in time can take centuries. Such time is immemorable.

For altered consciousness, time is not a something to be redeemed because it is lost, nor to be mastered because it enslaves, nor to be destroyed because it oppresses. Less is it a container of thought, passion, and sensation as the ocean is of fish. Time is the dimension of the altering force as it ruptures the reflection onto itself of consciousness, the gleaming knife edge of the present that severs the infinite to be from the infinite that has been. Temporal presence is the medium of percipience in that exchange, the discontinuity of one energy configuration with another, is the fuel of movement, or movement itself. Presence is the handing over and taking back, the addition and subtraction that make a difference, and being present to exchange is a way of speaking about participation in time. The reciprocal offering and receiving, receiving and offering, provides for the maintenance of inequalities, incomparabilities, and differences between beings. Reciprocity distributes goods (energies, materialities) over a whole network that respects individualities insofar as they participate globally. Maintenance (*mains*-tenance, keeping by hand) is a temporal dynamic, and the highly charged action of percipience speaks of the maintenance of the lower by the higher. To notice energy difference (Hume) is to grow aware of a matrix in which exchange is possible. "Lively" perception is the coarse matter of earth body being brought to life by subtle body.

With percipience, when somatic energies exchange with non-somatic ones, traditional accounts of perception by sympathy, the feeling of *with*ness, come into play. When Proclus notices that "the adepts of hieratic science take as their starting point the things of appearance and the sympathies they manifest among themselves and with the invisible powers," he refers to percipience.[13] Percipience is initiatory in the sense that consciousness is altered and made dynamic by exchange with "things of appearance" and enlarged and elevated by that with "the invisible powers." Initiation is always and everywhere initiation into the fact of obligation. The facticity of this fact lies in how it predates consciousness and intentionality. The fact of obligation differs from a debt I incur vis-à-vis autonomously, acting as an equal among equals, in that it sits above me, a Damoclean sword, ready to sever my life in two. Since it has been incurred by no choice of my own, no choice can be given with respect to answering it. That the loan may be recalled at any moment and the debt cancelled imperiously means that the fact of obligation precedes all obligation. Initiation concerns that which takes precedence and percipience is initiatory because it reveals the precedence of things. The exchange of one with the other—things or powers—provides consciousness with a sense of place, a sensitivity to the location of one's being within the hierarchic whole of existence. Sympathetic perception affects consciousness, not like a soothing balm, but in a radical and disruptive way.

In Proclus it is clear how percipience unveils a network of correspondences in which somatic awareness participates. There is no reason to believe that contact, the exchange of one inequality with another, is restricted to the human soma. Since any form of life is capable of working toward the maintenance of the whole, each exists under an imperative that obligates it specifically according to its form. The matrix of exchange, if made known to an unlimited consciousness, like Indra's net would have forms endlessly dancing in concert with each other. To human consciousness released from retentive grasping, portions of the matrix grow perceptible when touched by our own soma, and unveil themselves. Being made perceptible (the *percipi*), their life form is completed, raised to another level in the way that disclosure makes the knowable known. Discovery of the sympathies beings "manifest among themselves," making known the knowable, is, as Proclus claims, a starting point. It fulfills the terms of an uncreated obligation, the fact of which in creating consciousness, creates a debt of making the knowable known.

Sympathetic consciousness is, therefore, not an affective state that responds to obligations that govern a face-to-face situation, displaying an attentiveness to the other's need. That level of moral action is a result of freedom and intentionality and belongs by right to an autonomous equal among equals. An effect of contact, sympathy makes palpable the *with*ness that interrelates the inequalities among themselves and to the whole. Interconnecting channels of sympathy define the matter of exchange, one for the other, in such a way that when consciousness is contacted, the matrix becomes known. In being unveiled, consciousness shows itself a participant in a network of affinities and mutualities. As sympathy carries out its mission of sustenance, feeding the other, an integral, a "starting point," of maintenance is nearly manifest—a nonorigin beyond origins. Just as lower sustains higher by prayerful concern for the other, the higher turns toward the lower to honor its work of obligation.

The *sym-pathein*, the all-suffering, of sympathy refers to the work of exchange of an altered consciousness. Not a turn toward joy and effervescence (though these occur), its alteration lies in a recognition of a responsibility toward others that has arisen without choice. This is a responsibility already waiting to meet consciousness in the moment of its disrupted unrest, that consciousness steps into like a skin. It is there, there is no escape unless by refusal, negation of movement and alteration, the self-interest of property and sleep. A commitment that waits for the door to open, an obedience that cannot hear the word *no*, the demand of sympathy is not measured by a conscious willingness to take it on, but absolutely. Because consciousness is never done with the responsibility—because it is not *with* it in duration and because it cannot be done with—there is suffering. To suffer is to bear the incompleteness of contact in the knowledge of the completeness of the obligation. Inasmuch as the "work" of the work of exchange lies in percipience, in disclosure the matrix of life forms, the demand on consciousness is for knowledge. Knowledge of obligation is not that of transparency—the gaze beholding the visible realm—but of place, dependency, and need—invisible means of support. Such knowledge can be called "self-knowledge."

Percipience, the movement of consciousness into movement, does not exhaust discussion of the alteration of consciousness. Related to the hyletic flow, with or without the "I can" of kinaesthesis, consciousness in community with soma is in community with the nonsomatic world. This sensitivity, a kind of "sympathetic mediation" that Marcel has in mind, itself is liable to disruption—symmetrically since it arises within a breaking off of retentional consciousness. I am not thinking of the fact that since percipience is a dynamic equilibrium, a moving balance, it stumbles, spills, and is washed away, and that the object and its shadow [Ablauf] is again taken up. The petering out of disruptive influence is different from the refreshing of the impulse. The stop that concerns me at present comes as a subtle disruption of percipience itself in which somatic awareness is emptied of content without ceasing to be. In this case, there is percipience without specific correspondences. Affinities, similitudes, analogies, resemblances—the liking of like things in a dialectic of love—have no force or vivacity in the percipient impression. By contrast, somatically felt and sensately touched, consciousness registers the arc of percipience itself rather than a segment of it. It is as if emptied of specific claims on the foreground of attention, a background becomes apparent. Its vibratory curvature is that of subjectivity, understood not as the for-itself retentively holding on to its story of itself, but as the resonance of the arche name. "I am, I exist," whenever I am able to hear and to follow the vibration of the arche name. Listening, such as the soma is capable of, is essential if this project is to be realized.

That existential awareness is without content expresses what Marcel calls its "exclamatory quality." It says nothing and yet by virtue of its saying by not saying anything, cries out. The nothing not said is not nullity, vacancy, or zero. The plenitude of existence contrasts sharply with consciousness's paucity of options. Just as grammatically, exclamation is marked at the end of a statement, so too, the "I am" bears no record of its presence except that of its termination. Its echo is its signature. A memory that cannot be held, it remembers itself to itself and to the matrix that supports (and is supported by) it. The arche name is treasure hidden deep within the soma that cannot be brought to the surface by will since it precedes will and serves only that which takes precedence. When it resounds, however, the entire anarchaic dimension that cuts traumatically through consciousness discovers its meaning. The arche name reveals itself unique, a "one without a second," and therefore incomparable, indescribable, tremblingly ineffable.

Since hyletic awareness is still determinate (discerning specific currents of energy within the soma), indeterminacy comes as an inner disruption, a hiatus in the flux, a gap in the continuity of exchange. Unlike the erasure of the gap that resumption of objectification brings, existential awareness is an explosion rather than a collapse of energy potential. As if attention were suddenly directed to the source energy of forms, awareness of existence inverts the field and reveals what lies behind, nourishing specificities in their hiding and unveiling. Because the welling up of a background radiation, the epiphany of the field, overloads the circuitry of peripience, only the resulting blank—with its singular taste—offers consciousness data for exclamation.

In exclaiming, consciousness marks that "form is emptiness." Only in a paradoxical sense is the recognition a liberation. Existential awareness, in lying beyond the farthest limit of freedom, is a freedom from the freedom of consciousness. As long as consciousness is free to calm itself in the face of its obsessive fear of discontinuity, its freedom lies in its play, its repetitive loss (to fear) and recovery (to intention). Since freedom, the essence of the for-itself in its appropriation of the material of consciousness, forms the basis of an ethics of separateness, cessation of freedom frees consciousness to participate in the terrestial and cosmic community. More importantly, exclamation is the cry of responsibility. The "I am" that predates the fictional freedom of the for-itself bears witness to the fact of obligation. It recognizes that for the "loan" of its life, it must take up its specific task in maintenance of the life matrix. That specificity consists of the peculiar unveiling of reality through percipience, its body being an instrument of conscious disclosure. That I am bound by responsibility before I intentionally assume an obligation points to a responsibility to becoming responsible. Existential awareness, in revealing the "I am" as a co-responsible in maintaining the created order, reveals a cause for exclamation, not dejection. That creation has intrinsic goodness is an aspect of the revelation that lifts the burden of consciousness, straightens its back, and sends it uprightly forward to meet the world.

It follows that consciousness as constituted does not and cannot exhaust subjectivity. The limit given by Kant's statement that "pure *a priori* principles are indispensable for the possibility of experience," is a productivity limit.[14] Constitutive principles are indispensable only as long as they are retained for production purposes by the ego. Released from the need repeatedly to produce itself, consciousness swells to new limits that include intelligible objects even as ego shrinks to become a subordinate to soma. The obsession to constitute itself as well as the fear of cessation gives way spontaneously when the truth of self-limitation is felt. When limit ceases to limit itself, the limit that faces consciousness is different—is the different. To the extent that its being is given by difference, by an awakening through disruption, to that extent consciousness returns to limits set before its origination, its anarchaic limits. These limits are ethical in that they express themselves obligatorily. They limit consciousness like a skin, and like a skin, consciousness is born into their integument, their binding power, their ability to veil and unveil. The limits disclose themselves in disclosing the arche name, the name that consciousness is given at origin, advent, and arrival. The disclosure discloses that the arche name, the ownmost name of consciousness, also names the other. Being the other's name, "I am" calls forth a responsibility since whenever I call myself, I call myself forth to face the other—to ease his/her suffering, lighten his/her despair, and raise his/her hope. From beyond being, I am addressed by an imperative that can be answered only from within the skin of my being.

That the deeper reach of subjectivity lies beyond retention and memory, in the dynamic milieu of the soma, means, in Marcel's words, that we are not at our own disposal. We are unequal to ourselves. We do not coincide with who we are, and the remainder is something that we cannot grasp. The gathering of awareness—a re-membering—takes place through the exercise of consciousness, but the specific exertion is abandon, relinquishment, and release. To surrender intentionality for the sake of submitting ethically to what takes precedence requires the subject to pass over through continguity and opacity to the voice of the higher. Submission of the will ("Not my will, but Thine") can be taken on as a practice, but has no fore-ordained result. Consciousness willed into submission and subjectivity rounded out is accomplished by another's will. The face of the other presents itself disruptively and disturbingly in front of the self in order that the self forget itself. The other—beaten, tortured, despairing, wracked, broken—is simply the life of Hobbes's creature, "solitary, poor, nasty, brutish, and short," heard as the ethical call.

To hear the arche name, to hear the only name, the name that names the attributes of God, is to hear the name that I call myself. To hear percipiently is to be stunned into hearing, to be found wanting in hearing, which is obedience, for it is not to hear anything audible at all. It is not to hear a word sound but the hyle of a word sound. With the arche name, the limits of my skin reverberantly define a limit beyond consciousness. *That I am* splits apart the skin and opens it to a life body that is not only mine but also the other's. Consciousness bursts from a life body swollen with disclosure, and in a traumatized condition, finds itself reborn, a subject to a higher imperative that decrees the birth of consciousness itself. The deeper reach of subjectivity does not, therefore, belong to ontology since it is not a matter of being a subject (substance, substratum) but to ethics that treates being subject to conditionality and liability. As Kant foresaw (but here for very different reasons from Kant's), the "I am" cannot be discursively completed since it has a radical ethical contingency. The "I am" is not a ghost figure transcendentally and apperceptively shadowing experience—a memory I cannot quite remember—but as flesh and blood as my body is when I inhabit it. Because they are as different as necessity and contingency, subjectivity and the arche name are not interchangeable like suits of clothing. The difference, the sliver of incongruence, is source of a recurrent disruption to consciousness. That I do not fit my name or my name me—like a mirror image fits a face—is an irritant, a goad, a nagging thought, a prick of consciousness, and may be the grain of sand that seeds a pearl. The "I am" is a necessary being while subjectivity is strife, risk, challenge, loss, and attainment. The effort to recall myself to a name that is and has been reserved for me since before created time is to heed the cry of necessitation. It is the effort to uncover an ethical core of consciousness that has become encrusted with increasingly dead layers of being.

Ethics is upsurge, Alcibiades barging in to break up a nice symposium on love. Discourse has moved from the mortal to the immortal and is about to assimilate the mystery of desire when discord storms in unannounced. Eruptive, an electric current passes through consciousness to recall it from dialectic to the supreme but undialectical achievement, to what takes precedence. The unprecedented casts the torn fabric of being aside and reminds consciousness of a transaction which consciousness did not witness: the conceiving of its own obligation. The "fear and trembling" that attends an unnegotiated pact is entirely unlike that of a social contract. It is other than the for-itself's trying to acomplish its own measure through project making and problem solving. That subjectivity can fall short of an issue beyond its understanding fuels a sense of injustice and impotence that may yet serve the memory of the immemorial. That the subject is judged by a measure that is other, by the measure of the other, can rupture a self-complacence of contingency. To shed the Protagorean and humanistic mantle for an ethical nakedness reveals a human destiny that leads beyond humanity.

Does it follow that the *who* of the primal question, "Who am I?" cannot be known by consciousness? Discourse, a semantic descriptor, an exhaustive list of properties inhering in prime matter: these formulae yield traces or relics. Familiar products of decomposition, they excite a longing for the present in a consciousness accustomed to the past. To reject any single trace as incongruent with the life within the life body and to accept as a task a search for completeness is a human response to discovery. Who I am cannot be said, but to leave it unsaid is to abrogate the role of speaker. In the effort, the discontinuity of obligation and discharge of obligation speaks the *who* more articulately than human voice can. To meet its lack in the face of the other—reticence, aversion, closure—is to meet the *who* that would give up its place to the unknown *I* and live again. In the suffering face of the other, consciousness meets the *who,* its own ethical imperative to remember that from whose hand it once had sprung.

6

DIGRESSION ON PROJECTIVE GEOMETRY

The genius of Euclidean geometry is to provide a frame for visual space, a light-filled realm in which distance equals transparency. Just as the eye apparently sees in accordance with geometrical law as it beholds the physical world, so too, the mind's eye, the lumen naturale, works geometrically. On closer examination, Euclid's discovery, under the banner of truth, functions as ideology to perpetuate the hegemony of intellect. Geocentrism becomes a way of discounting aspects of subjectivity that are proximate, opaque, and nonvisual. Since that which cannot be accommodated by the trope of spatial (meaning, Euclidean) coordinates is inordinately nonexistent and suffers pangs of nonbeing, its ontological inferiority must forever cloud a philosophical concern with it.

The purity of pure mathematics allows a disinterest with regard to perception and an interest in developing sound and consistent alternatives to Euclid's geometry. Among the non-Euclidean models that the nineteenth century developed is its direct inverse, projective (synthetic or planar) geometry. Projective geometry grounds an exploration of somatic space in rigor and demonstrates that the counterintuitive nature of spatial relations of the soma must not be geometrically discounted.

Projective geometry begins with the polarity of point and plane, but unlike Euclid, does not abandon the dynamic exchange between poles in favor of one or the other. Since it does not fixate on the point and fix the plane at infinity (as does Euclidean geometry), the movement between outer and inner, disembodied and embodied, and earthly and celestial is not destroyed. Because the passage between polarities is the space-creative process, projective geometry discloses space-in-becoming and is diachronic rather than synchronic. In disclosing the signification of becoming spatial and passing out of spatial existence, the new geometry locates the "gateway of manifestation" beyond ontology, transparency, presence, and representation. It demonstrates how inspiration draws from the infinite and, in emptying out, expires unto the infinite. In addressing the becoming of becoming, it thereby allows the space of a breath between the sign and its signification.

Although projective geometry respects the polar balance between point and plane, it dynamically derives the former from the latter. In the case of Euclid's axioms, a plane is generated by an infinite extension of a point in two dimensions. A line mediates between point and plane inasmuch as it is the one-dimensional extension of a point. In projective geometry, an infinite plane in its totality, by contrast, is a single whole, fluid and intensive. "A plane is that which has no parts." It is the undivided and indivisible entity, portions of which may be represented as tabletops and ballgrounds, but which extends to infinity in all directions in a self-enclosed and almost cyclic manner. A point, on the other hand, is the intersection of an infinite number of planes (figure 3). To go out to infinity in one direction is to return from infinity in the opposite direction.

There is, moreover, only a single point at infinity. To go leftward to infinity is to come to the same point as one finds going rightward. Since the same is true with a vertical approach, nadir equals zenith in the pure space of projective geometry.

With regard to the plane in its totality, the figure it traces at infinity is not a circle but a straight line. Although it surrounds our space on all sides, the line-at-infinity is straight. Correspondingly, for the whole of space, the circumference or totality of infinitely

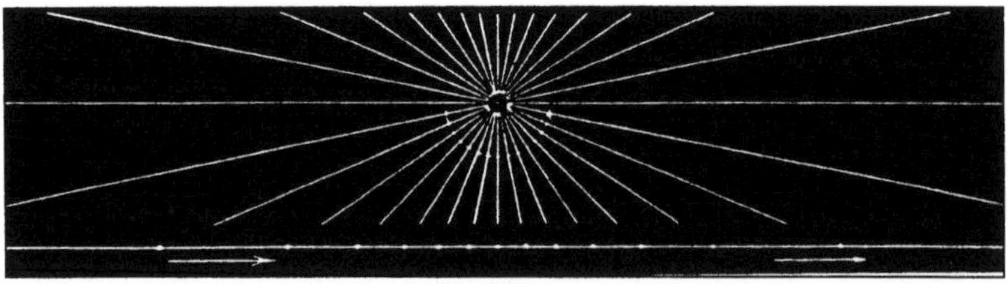

Figure 3

distant points is not a sphere (not even Erigena's sphere, whose center is everywhere and circumference nowhere) but a plane. The plane-at-infinity curves back on itself, self-enclosingly. Euclid's geometry, moreover, appears as a special case of this all-embracing interplay of point and plane. If we single out from among the infinity of planes one that is "infinitely distant" and fix it as the absolute periphery of cosmic space, then we derive the familiar results of optical geometry.

Because it carries the principle of duality to its logical conclusion, projective geometry provides a counterbalance to the disequilibrium of perspectival geometrics, with its overemphasis on the visible. Sight, we saw, implies contraction, focus, and retentivity. A field of vision is gathered and positioned in a pointlike manner on the surface of the retina. The implication is that every spatial point is a potential eye point, able to gather unto itself the forms of surrounding space. Each point, as an eye point, is the apex of a cone of light rays that, by optical construction, originates with the object and terminates at the eye's surface (figure 4). Replacing contraction with expansion, focus with defocus, we can, however, redraw the Euclidean picture-in-a-plane in terms of a projective one. Take the lines radiating from the object's surface and in conjunction with the eye point, convert them into planes. Then take the points on the object's surface from which the lines originate and in conjunction with the eye point, convert them to lines. Now the picture-in-the-plane, formerly composed of lines and points, has become a corresponding composition of planes and lines in the eye point. An extended entity (picture-in-the-plane) has thereby been received intensively in the point. If a new plane is placed before the eye point, a new picture will appear, isomorphic to the original but corresponding to the relative position of the new plane (figure 5). In this fashion, the spatially creative operation of projective geometry can be illustrated.

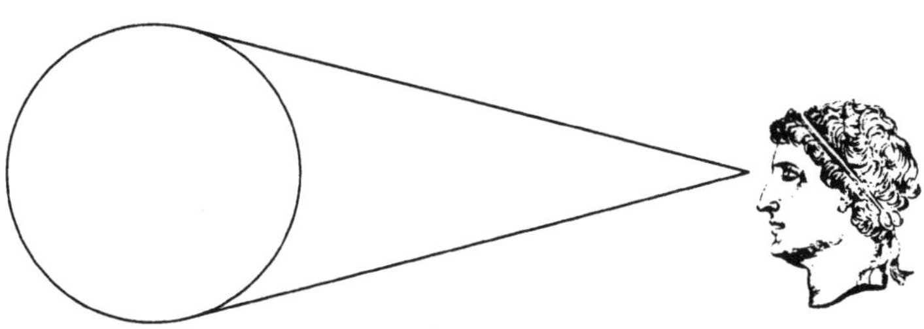

Figure 4

Figure 5

As long as spatial intuition is defined, as Kant does, in terms of optical, Euclidean geometry, the consequences of projective geometry will seem counterintuitive. When we open intuition toward the soma, opacity, contact, and movement, the "antispace" properties of projective geometry vanish. One property has to do with the way that visual space is centrically organized in terms of Cartesian coordinates (two perpendicular axes radiating from an origin.) Physical forces—gravitation, magnetism, electricity, radioactivity—obey the law of the spatial center, beginning intensely at origin and losing energy along a radial movement toward the periphery. As in an explosion, such events begin at ground zero and move outward toward the absolute or cosmic plane that Euclid has fixed as a final boundary. If we invert Euclid's postulates, projective space appears with the impact of an opaque intuition. Instead of a cosmic plane, substitute a cosmic point; instead of an infinite periphery, substitute an infinite center. In the newly created space, energies move inwardly from relative peripheries toward the absolute center. Rather than expansion, decay, and dilution in the vast circumference of optical space, events in the new space perpetually tend toward contraction, renewal, and concentration in the vast center of projective space. Invisible lines of influence that arise at the outskirts, the perimeter, the outer limits, touch the interior of events and ineluctably direct their course toward the vanishing point of proximity. Furthermore, since each line of influence, taken in conjunction with the "event point," constitutes a new plane, we have the creative inversion of space that I illustrated above. In projective space, peripheral forces directed toward "event points" as their center, absolute and infinite, sustain and nourish that which takes place because such events are perceived as the potential of the future. Events are the point foci of peripheral forces that are engaged in a process of becoming spatial.

One further property of projective or "anti"space is worth mentioning. Just as centric forces expand to fill space with ever-increasing dilutions of an original potency, so inversely do peripheral forces empty space with ever-increasing concentrations of a non-originary potency. The first involves gravitational phenomena, the second, those of lightness. As the latter move inward toward the cosmic or absolute point, projective space hollows out and grows more rarefied even though matter condenses. As an approximate example, if we imagine a sphere, then that which is optically the infinite, empty space outside the surface is projectively the finite volume. Conversely, that which is optically the finite volume (interior to the surface) is projectively the empty space that tends toward the infinite emptiness of the cosmic point.

The action of a force that operates in projective space is then the inverse of that in optical space. Such a force arises at the periphery, on the outside of the cosmic sphere, and works inward toward the cosmic point woven of many planes. In this movement, as the radius (measured optically) grows smaller, the projective sphere grows larger. That which is nearer (in optical terms) is that which is farther away, projectively speaking. The vanishing point is not of the infinitesmal but of the infinitely immense. Nor does it represent absolute contraction, that into which gravitation pulls all things, a supreme density. The center, formed by a manifold of planes and containing the volume of the whole sphere, is absolute lightness and the totality of expansiveness evoked by peripheral forces—a negative gravity.

Projective space provides a "grid" for somatic awareness, a kind of inversion of Euclidean consciousness. Although my sketch is incomplete, at least two consequences of the balanced polarity of projective geometry function in the soma. The paradoxical notions that proximity is distance and that force moves from periphery to center help spatialize the opaque contact that surrounds the gate of altered consciousness. That alteration itself represents a geometrical inversion (in the sense explained above) and suggests a conception of the other as altered space. If projective geometry geometrizes the becoming-spatial, then passage through the gate, from somatic awareness to optical consciousness, concerns the rigidification of forms. Fixing a single plane from the infinity of planes at infinity, stipulating it as the cosmic plane, optical consciousness abandons the rhythm intrinsic to projective space—that between point and plane. Forgetting that peripheral forces hollow out the space at the center, optical consciousness represents time as running on and running out and dwells in loss and decay. Prevented from entering the phenomenal world, the rejuvenating, creative energy of space languishes, cut off from consciousness deep within the human soma.

III

TRANSFORMATION

ARGUMENT

Disruption is the temporalization of difference. It is the anarchaic in the sense that it comes from a time that is or never has been present, hence is unrepresentational. It leaves no memory trace. Likewise, disruption does not belong to *Dasein*, the realm of spatiotemporal phenomena. It manifests as a wound in time, in consciousness's felt vulnerability to forgetfulness, lethe. In the cessation of self-production (the ego), consciousness is returned to a wholeness that objectification, its obsession, erases. It willingly turns from its project of signifying the various phenomena of its own creation, a discourse on the essences it sympathetically receives from impassive being. Initially, discourse is a product of active imagination, but similarity is soon replaced by sameness. The project of objectivity, a vast net of meanings that protects consciousness from the other, also obscures the real essence of itself from itself. The arche name *I* makes its appearance in the throes of disruption, and so is essentially nondisclosed and nondisclosable. Since disruption comes from the higher, *I* is the first name of what takes precedence.

In the creative wind

incredible cosmic command

to sever,

Disjoin, separate, break—

death in the world.

—Hayden Carruth, "The Sleeping Beauty"

7

THE INTERVAL

When each thing clashes with the other—Empedocles's world—an interrupted state is meant where end is broken off from middle, middle rent from beginning, and beginning being torn asunder. Fruition denied, perfection absconded, completeness overruled, accomplishment compromised: these portray a fracture that gives rise to a double attitude. Futility and nihilism are, by a thin membrane, separated from hope and realism, yet if a spark of initiative is present, signification can be discovered in the preprimal condition of abrasion. Intervals of susceptibility during which interruption is magnetically attracted define the temporality of each thing. An interval is the duration of influx. The specifics of influence impress themselves, lending altered tempo, rhythm, tone, melody, texture, and substance to the original march. Change, the only unchangefulness, rules each thing but not continuously. The interval is temporalization of change while between intervals inertia and habit preside.

In Empedocles's vision, time operates within specific epochs and finds its own tempo within that epoch. The works of time ("mortal things") are brought to an end at the end of a temporal epoch by *eris*. Eris—disruptive force—opposes that which impels time in a creative direction—eros—that brings about relatively stable and independent configurations of energy. Viewed through a logic of sameness, the difference in temporalization is lost since this hermeneutic sets eris and eros equal and opposite to one another, forces that interaction within the same vast incomprehensible container. Empedocles expresses his thought through visual and spatial tropes when he says:

> When *eris* has fallen into the lowest depths of the vortex, *eros* has reached the center, into it do all things come together so as to be only one, not all at once but gradually from different quarters, and as they come *eris* retires to the extreme boundary . . . in proportion as it runs out *eros* in a soft immortal boundless stream runs in.[1]

The image signifies two separate, interpenetrating gyres or cones whose relative motions determine the "continual shifting" of things, a state of integrity or disintegration. When motion of eros increases, motion of eris diminishes, and so on, and so on (figure 5). Heraclitus's phrase, "dying each other's life, living each other's death," resounds as a declaration of equality of the living and the dying.

When we dispel the illusions of sameness that cast Love and Strife as protagonist and antagonist that share the same stage, temporality reappears. The scene is occupied by eros who in mid-sentence is disrupted by eris. Strife is arisen, time is no longer the same. Time now belongs to the interval, discontinuity dispatches the community of eros, and the primal anarchaic force, the force that negates order, measure, and the running off [Ablauf] of time, crushes all things. The interval is cataclysm, catastrophe, apocalypse (all Greek words), Hamlet's mill, final destruction, finality of finality. It is not more of the same, in the modes of receding, subsiding, easing, ebbing, lessening, weakening, diminishing, decaying, decomposing. Where equality in opposition binds eris to eros, a hermeneutic reveals the projection of retentivity at work, a consciousness that reads its own worst fears of sinking down [Hinabsinken] into the life of phenomena. By constrast, catastrophic finality ends the ending. No passing away, past claims on being are already silenced and through the shattering endurance of eris, no present claim has been voiced. The slate has been wiped clean, the blank, Locke's tabula rasa, is ascendent. In that time (*in illo tempore*), time has withdrawn from a ceaseless repetition of the same and again has enfolded itself to the advent of the different. Time forgets its amnesia and remembers its immemorial memory. Eris breaks upon the shoals of lethe, beckoning with what is higher.

Where suppleness and agility lend consciousness an adaptability, a way to regain its footing from influx to influx, continuity is preserved. To recover itself after a feared loss due to interruption—the knock on the door—requires continual narration: the narrator on retainer. In the story that tells itself, stoppage is dissolved in the telling and becomes nonexistent. The monster at the gate, Cerberus, is illusory, untruth, fictive, and can be dismissed. As long as knowledge of the interval remains hidden, recovery reinforces a dream of creation that creates itself, an automatic creation, a creation by an antonomous, self-creating self, by minimizing dependency and obsession. Sui generis, the ego is obligated to no other except by its own will. By contrast, knowledge of the interval signifies a release from a self-making, self-retaining character woven into consciousness. No dialectic of love, it is a nondialectical acceptance of eris.

The grinding, grating teeth of disruption, Cerberus's maw, clamp willy-nilly down on the works of things, consciousness's tragic attempt to gain persistance in time. The usual rendition of Empedocles's double tale, moreover, offers little by way of consolation since the return of eros, Timaeus's outer sphere that the Maker left unaltered, is the resumption of the autonomous will and its denial of the obligatory other. Alternation (of Love with Strife) replaces alteration of consciousness. When marginalization of the disrupting force recurs, the void in consciousness is again avoided and with it, a more inclusive, ethical will. A more helpful hermeneutic gives a different signification to Empedocles. When "all the god's limbs in turn began to quake," a new epoch, an epoch in the interval between recorded epochs, is proclaimed.[2] Though its contents leave no memory trace (because they are never present to a retentive consciousness), the split in the continuum of epochs holds a key to the destiny of human consciousness. With cessation of the erotic bond of the for-itself, on the catwalk between the double ramparts (the inter-val), an altered consciousness can perform.

The epochal crack between temporal epochs, separate equalities of the same time, can be discerned in Husserl's poetic description of brackets. The bracket is a textual or typographical mark [used to enclose matter] in a parenthesis, that is, to make an (insertion) by way of amplification, explanation, or digression. As such, to place in brackets, to invoke the parenthetical, is to indicate a departure from the thematizing of discourse. Bracketing is a double action, both leavestaking [of the current theme] and homecoming [to the inserted matter]. Since to place in brackets, to make an insertion of "this entire natural world," is to insert it in another text, an alteration of consciousness is assumed to preside.[3] The self-originating origin, erotic self-liking, objectification, and the autonomous will do not vanish like a wisp of smoke, but inserted elsewhere or nowhere, cease to act on the text under prime focus. Although brackets both extract and add in [Descartes's text on doubt in the *Meditations* being the second, as is this short text], the bracketing of consciousness does not have the intent to insert it in another place, but to neuter, pacify, tranquilize, and isolate it. Through bracketing, objectifying consciousness will be added to nowhere and will be parenthetical to no other text. Like a memory continually on the verge of retrieval, consciousness waits, a suspended act of insertion into itself, a self-insertion. Husserl's brackets seem turned in on themselves, introverted, [bracketing] what already constitutes a distinct epoch and not facing that which differentiates the epochal quality of time. The brackets need to reverse themselves, do an about-face, go the other way:] [. Then, while they enclose "any judgment that concerns spatiotemporal existence (Dasein)," they simultaneously define the epoche itself.[4] The fissure, that which disjoins adjacent times *in* brackets and, therefore, must remain *outside* them, is, however, not timeless but of a different time. When the temporalization of difference, the temporal interval, arrives, appointment—judgment, memory, loss, recovery—is suspended the way a timetable is due to a natural disaster.

That the break in time, a right-hand bracket closing the insertion prior to a left-hand bracket opening another insertion, breaks memory the way a supercharge overloads an electric circuit. When memory of running off and sinking down stop, memory of trauma floods the awareness with its being. Traumatic memory is the immemorable, the amnestic. Since it is memory that does not retain the time *of* wounding (that time has ceased), it remembers a time of difference. A concealed truth, a childhood injury, a biased judgment, a denying attitude: the surfacing of trauma gives pause to the time of self-constitution because consciousness is face to face with the wound itself. In the moment that consciousness is reminded of its presumptive self-origination, of its illusion of bursting fully clothed from the head of Zeus, it remembers its wounded condition. Time, the inner form of intuition, itself is wounded because consciousness assumes the role of its creator. Traumatized time, time that obsessively fears disruption, that runs off in flight from unanticipated disruption, is in need of healing. When that which takes precedence reminds consciousness of its wound—its unbirthed trauma—a time of healing is nigh. The temporalization of difference, time when the brackets face away and nothing is to be inserted, is a time of greatness, when the great overwhelms the small, world-avoiding artistry of the ego.

If thematization and discourse are to rediscover their magical potency, acceptance of wounded time must occur. Within the epoch-making brackets, *acceptance* is a term among terms, replaceable by sameness and synonomy, accepting equals. Consciousness represents the idea of consent and receipt in terms of agreement. Acceptance places consciousness in agreement with itself and is therefore an act of becoming congruent to its own constituting powers, empowering its own constitution, constituting itself. When the retraumizing disruption breaks through and the wound is felt, consciousness remembers its obligation to repay the loan of itself, its borrowed life and liveliness, and accepts responsibility for making payment. Since to heal wounded time means to unclench the grip of memory on time, acceptance requires an about-face with respect to disruption. In being obligated to accept that it does not self-originate, that moment by moment its recreation lies with a source different from itself, consciousness is called to face the other. The call exists because difference makes it imperative. It is neither gentle nor ungentle. To bear witness to how the other's suffering—fear, rage, self-pity, resentment, greed, poverty—wounds time is to accept time's woundedness. It is to work at repaying the debt that trauma incurs, the nonacceptance, obsession, and self-love (self-eroticism) that come to substitute for the term of time.

Eris breaks and consciousness ebbs away like blood from a mourner's face: this is a nightmare. The human fear of the still point of disruption projects loss rather than accepts movement. The time between epochal time is upheaval in that consciousness is altered by contact with difference. Since within the soma lies an organ of perception by which to recognize the other, time between insertions, a noninserted time, is somatic temporality. In the split second when the millstone of strife grinds love's castles to sand, percipience is receptivity to an emanation from the higher. Consciousness remembers that which, having no concern with "spatiotemporal existence (Dasein)," the being of thought or desire, or theories of origin, accepts its brokenness in time as well as the responsibility of repayment. Trembling, it accepts an obligation "without recourse," one that cannot be rescinded or qualified, that lays upon consciousness like an atmosphere. Since obligation in this context implies initiation into obligation, consciousness is under surveillance to remember and embody the alteration. Since the imperative necessitates ceasing to be itself and becoming other, the ethical (as Kant and Husserl suggest) is a nonnatural supposition. It is rejection of self-identity and obedience unto death whereas consciousness's natural state is autoreproduction and eroticism. Only the dejected, pitiful, downcast, wan face of the other—the person beside me, my neighbor, the one the television camera zeroes in on—only her or his suffering face has the power to break through my self-ness and remind me of the schism in time. Only that face that can wound can heal since only through the wound does healing occur.

The interval ruins ruination. Time's running off as well as phenomena's inevitable decay are cut short by . . . whoever calls me from completing this sentence. Because it is uncompleted, I am still under sentence, not having finished my term, hoping for pardon but unfree. Whoever interrupts me draws me up short, face to face with an obligation that predates this sentence or any I could complete. In the moment of time's standstill abides another time, less quiescent, more explosive. Through its detonation, the cells of my body are reacquainted with a wholeness that makes a somatic whole whole, an integral beyond the integrity of altered consciousness. At a cellular level, neither form nor deformation has a voice but only the utter relativity of form and nonform. Both rise and fall together, like a twilight and a dawn. If the plasmic condition can be said, the saying has to do most relevantly with a liberation that is a gain. There is the lesser liberation, freeing consciousness from self-love, its erotic autoproduction, and its wound, which, though the lesser because it is negative is no less important to transact than the greater. The greater or second liberation presumes the first in that it posits the freedom to take a responsible place within creation. A creative will and a continuing work of creation, submission and participation, both speak in the compassionate touch, a gentle pressure on the grieving other's arm. The greater liberation concerns transformation, the transforming of the lead of suffering into the gold of affirmation. This is empowerment to stand with disruption, not to be repulsed by the other's mourning but to wield with disruptive power—a bracket turned the other way—the compassionate strength that rejuvenates the source.

The sacred hush of the stop: is this the starting point of hieratic science that Proclus has in mind, whose adepts observe "that all things form a whole"? Such notation cannot belong to a consciousness whose temporal mode is running off, that is, a successive, sequential continuum of now instants. Wholeness for objectifying consciousness is a result of inductive inference plus the privileged position of the gaze: location at time *x* that is outside of the continuity of time slices. "All things in a temporal whole" expresses perception from a time dimension more inclusive and energic than that which sinks down [Hinabsinken]. Because time between closed sets of brackets, time of fission, takes in more during its day, one breath is a human lifetime. The effect—elevation, height, altitude, verticality—neutralizes the autoreproduction and self-love of consciousness and lets it dwell as altered in relation to the other. Time that is a dying away itself has been exploded, giving a meaning to death that consciousness with its obsession altogether lacks. The other's death, in that moment, takes precedence because without the other, there is no sense to life. Death is the nonobligatory end to obligation, the sting of which—like a task uncompleted—goads us toward awakening in this life.

8

OBJECTIVITY AND MEANING

Consciousness under the reign of retentivity is defined by Locke as the keeper of "signs of internal conceptions."[1] Since they are a species of Ablaufsphanomene, perishable and prone to decomposition, ideas or terms of meaning must be held onto: the charge of memory or reproductive imagination. Persecuted by a fear of its own lapsing, consciousness sets the risk that accompanies lethe, or forgetting, incredibly high. The "perfect ignorance," imbecility or madness, that waits to devour the mind can be outwitted only by perfect memory, letting no signs go. For consciousness, there is no sleep even during sleep lest it wake an idiot or a fool, which is to say, in a living death. In sleep, in dreams, there is the continued work of the imagination as it rehearses its terms of meaning. So effective is the practice of meaning that in dream life, as Descartes's bewilderment of the *Meditations* confirms, no difference separates consciousness from consciousness, dream from waking:

> even if these general kinds of things, eyes, head, hands, and so on, could be imaginary, at least it must be admitted that some simple and more universal kinds of things are real and are as it were the real colors out of which there are formed in our consciousness all our pictures of real and unreal things.[2]

Consciousness and "universal kinds of things" or "signs of internal conceptions" mutually imply one another, or better, as a smile signifies joy, meaning signifies consciousness. Since apprehension that a smile signifies nothing, that signification has been displaced, is consciousness's obsession with the lapse, nonmeaning equals with the nonconscious. In shock, stunned, dazed, stupified, the for-itself—the impersonal one—has the taste of the heart's stopping. When the moment-by-moment repetition of signs that is the heart of "spatiotemporal existence" (Dasein) stops, the abyss opens to swallow conscious life. A wary time, the interval.

The vigor of the pool of available signs—"universal kinds of things"—is in direct proportion to the vigor of memory. The more consciousness co-responds to that which evokes response in it, the more life the sign contains plus the wider the range of signs. As memory is strengthened, a plethora of signs prevails. As it weakens, as Plato notes concerning written signs, the number of signs diminishes and things can no longer be called to remembrance "from within themselves," but only with the aid or supplement of external marks. Further debilitation requires still more consolidation, the invention of schemes, networks, frameworks, outlines, tables, and algorithms—ways of weaving warp and woof of signs together into one graspable whole. Since the forgetting is then constrained by the strength of weave, the fabric of memory is at less risk of unraveling. As memory grows more deficient and the net more interwoven, more tautly its own self, signs cease referring or being a supplement to things within themselves and take on their own life. In a consciousness that is autoproductive, signs are substitutes exclusively for other signs, "pen" to "stylus" to "writing implement." Objectified entities, referents of signs, replace things that are consigned to a transcendental realm. Contact has become vacuous, and since nature abhors a vacuum, unnatural, mysterious, occult.

In a consciousness qualified by an infirm memory, meaning is the self-reflection of one sign in another, a glint of light the gaze casts that passes from one mirror to the next. Because terms have been multiplied such that many ideas represent the same object, substitution by synonomy becomes an ideal avenue through which meaning is conveyed. Synonomous meaning further exhausts a field of meaning that begins in a depleted state. Multiple sayings that signify the same (Bertrand Russell's "definite descriptions") help pin down an object, which is the substitute for the sum of its predicates and lacks a true nominative.[3] The fact that an object is missing a name, has no real essence but merely a nominal one, means that at best an object is pronominal, a he, she, or it. Gendered or not, *it* holds a place for a name that will never be. *It* is resigned to vacuity, to being a continual subtraction in order that nothing be in its place. Being absolutely without specificity, *it* is of perfect and absolute universality. Yet, having no face, suffering, or responsibility, *it* is as far from a "universal kind of thing" as *it* is from particularity, as far from death as from life. *It*, the oneself, is a neither/nor, a third something that robs from being and nonbeing alike. *It* is the perfectly unique objective, the suit of clothes that fits everyone, a nonexistence that can stand in for existence, a logical charade, dialectical pantomime, and ontological mimickry.

In a consciousness where memory can never be but deficient—object consciousness—*it* or the oneself is the substitute of substitution. Inasmuch as it fills in for consciousness, consciousness is identified with the oneself, the for-itself is a for-oneself. The rules of identification and reidentification (criteria) by which consciousness discerns phenomena rule it. *It* itself is given by a rule, the rule of the logical subject *x*: "no entity without identity." We say, of each thing *x* that serves as subject that its identity is given in its predicate F. Thus, *x* is F, Fx, e.g., "Socrates is mortal," becomes "X is Socrates such that it is mortal" or "The snake is a rope" becomes "X is a snake such that it is a rope." *It*, however, remains an unentitative entity since all the terms that build its identity are in the accusative. Whenever in response to its namelessness, its sheer nominalism—its pronominal accusation—*it* thinks to, *it* calls itself "I," ego. The "I am" or *sum* of Descartes is a grammatical statement that upon parsing makes no sense because it makes no claim to existence. Since what is meant is that *x* has I-like properties, that *it* looks like a subject, that *it* can pass for a subject as a mere reproduction can pass for a Rembrandt, existence is glossed over. When subjectivity is reduced to facsimile, autoreproduced, everywhere one and the same, consciousness is in subjugation, in subjunction. Subjunctive consciousness is by its declension contrary to fact, subbornly resisting actuality, preferring to be contingent to being per se. *It* is the subject thrown under the wheels of positivism, made vassal to logicians' whimsy, and driven back from the ethical response that claims both its humanity and its greater-than-humanity.

Substitution is sacrifice of subjectivity to the lower. When subjectivity is represented in the accusative, by predication, it, like a slave, is deemed no longer worthy to stand accused. A mere commodity, produced by the autoproduction or replication of consciousness, it is equally dispensable. Why bother to point a finger at a throwaway? When the lower is served by subjectivity, a door to what takes precedence is shut and bolted. As the framework of signs, related by rules of substitution and synonomy, is testament to the ego's wariness toward the lapse, so representational meaning itself is a defense against future rupture. With substitution the rule that admits no exceptions, the exceptional event of disruption is eo ipso outlawed. The vacancy of the name's place, expressed in Nietzsche's denial of God and substance, cannot be brought before the tribunal of the other since the oneself acknowledges no suffering other than its own. The face of the name having been effaced, the grotesque of the substitute now stares down the meaning of itself: self-destruction.

Sacrifice to the lower places the subject under objective rule, the rule of equals, a *demos* of terms. Meaning shifts entirely to the accusative and consists entirely in being assigned to a class. The group, set, collection, assembly, or coterie bears a name that rests equally upon all members, but because members belong to classes and not classes to members, the name belongs specifically to none. Although a shared name, no single member can claim its share independently and take its leave. Although in the logical independence of one subject from another is a nominal dependence, a totalitarianism of nomenclature, there is a freedom from care. Within the facelessness of the class, beneath the iron rule of the name, equals can legitimately replace equals, and this creates an illusion of movement. All entities that bear predicate F can be in place of *x*, the subject. Objectivity consists in the act of freeing the subject, the entity, from the weight of essence and by abstraction displaying it in its weightlessness by rule of synonomy. We can recall Locke's manifesto in this connection, that

> though we know not the real essences of things, all we can do is to collect such a number of single ideas as, by examination, we find to be united together in things existing, and thereof to make one complex idea. Which though it be not the real essence of any substance that exists, is yet the specific essence to which our name belongs.[4]

Far from seeing itself as a resignation, objectivity views itself as a boon and an advance. Objectivity does away with an intrusion into the being of the subject, its "real constitution," by assuming the matter of constituting itself: first, by providing a representative, and second, by assembling representatives of like subjects under the banner of equality. Maintaining the singularity of the subject by aborting an investigation into it, objectivity gives an advance absolution of the subject's blame or guilt. The burden of the subject, to unveil the unique *who*, the just essence, is lifted by objective rules since justice can be adjudicated by reference to procedure, as it were, out of court.

Objectivity, the freeing of the subject from subjection to essence, has the further virtue of quantifying being. Existence, the impredicable, cannot stand in the accusative since it itself is the matter of accusation. Objectivity shows that the subject whose existence is under accusation and has been charged to repay the loan of its creation bears no special, intrinsic mark of being, no scarlet letter or yellow star. Although objectivity acknowledges a distinction, in the subject itself, there is no difference between "Socrates speaks" and "Socrates exists." Difference, like subjectivity itself, is indicated by a sign that is not (again like subjectivity) a name but a functional operator. While "Fx" designates "Socrates speaks," "(x)Fx" designates "Socrates exists": "There is an *x* such that it is Socrates, and that *x* exists." Although the existential function "(x)" has a different mathematical operation than predication, the effect is the same. By assignation, a subject is given a name, and so too does it gain existence. Reducing being and naming to assignation, objectivity states its objection to the excessive burden of subjectivity—the goad of obligation and the ceaseless call of the other. The sting of real essence, the pain of death and life, never impresses the subject's skin since the subject is a substanceless shadow in the *polis* of the predicate.

Though liberation is a value, liberation by objectivity has costs not covered by assignation and assumption when consciousness becomes the constitutive principle of essence. Essence ceases to be deontological and becomes merely ontological when it "relates to a sort and supposes a species."[5] The advantages of confining being to the being of nomenclature and relegating real essence to, as Locke suggests, supposition are offset by the deficit. What is essential no longer resonates with the quest for precedence (what is highest) but acquiesces to precedent (what is past). Inasmuch as essence merely makes reference to the has-been, not to a disruption of the ongoing, it grows self-referential. Sorts and species are products of consciousness constituting the story of itself, its loss and recovery, the abyss of time, obsessive avoidance, and love of continuity. When an essential function of consciousness—representation—is set equal to essence per se, equality overrules essence at the expense of difference. Primary contact with the other-than-consciousness is sacrificed on the altar of certainty since the touch of disruption is brusque, unpredictable, and laden with risk. Because "real essence" speaks to the ear of submission, its loss implies a deafness to the facticity of obligation. Altered by the essential touch of things, their quiddity and suchness, consciousness recalls the imperative that preceeds essence: to render help to the other who disrupts my self-absorbed reverie by his/her tortured cry for mercy.

The promise in shifting from nominalism to essentialism fails, we shall see, to come to fruition. Essentialism affirms the singular contact with essence that a consciousness not bounded by autoproduction can attain. Impelled to movement by the presence of the world, consciousness is not limited by categories ("sorts" and "species") designed through motives of self-interest to keep it secure from disruptive memory. It is thereby able to seek essence in its concealment, enboldened by a belief in its own power of percipience. Consciousness informed by a somatic logos moves in the community of essence and communicates with the real constitution of things. "Since nothing is so secret or hidden," Paracelsus writes, "that it cannot be revealed, everything depends on the discovery of those things which manifest the hidden."[6] To raise essence from the ground of being and let it stand forth is to face the task of deciphering the marks that follow essence to its burial place. Essence is not quiescence until it coincides perfectly with its place of being, subsides, and is absorbed in the plenum. Prior to subsidence and interiorization, as it is pulled by the gravitational force of being, essence spews marks, figures, and traits of itself, just as a comet develops a tail in its fall toward the sun. These nonaccidental excrescences or products of turbulence remain even after essence has come to rest, engulfed by the unmanifest. In the poetic figure of essentialism, they form the text visible that indicates the road to discovery of the text invisible. More flamboyantly, Paracelsus:

> We men discover everything that lies hidden in the mountains by external signs and correspondences. . . .

> There is nothing that nature has not signed in such a way that man may discover its essence.[7]

That the meanings divulged by essence are evidential shows essentialism's affinity to objectivity. Since contact with essence is unmediated by objective language or a self-constituting consciousness, essentialism differs from objectivity in that subjectivity is not equated with ego. Subjectivity is an inequality that arises when essence is pried up from the ground of being and let stand forth. As an inequality in exile from the rule of equals (objectivity), the subject is sensitive to, is percipient of, the difference that marks each thing and each thing from the other. The anarchaic disposition itself is an engine of discernment as it works to break up the recalcitrant, inertial retentivity of the for-itself. When the subject is expanded by the hyletic flow and kinaesthesis, its evidence does not derive from a substitution of itself for itself nor from rules of translation and synonomy nor from the lexical entries for several representational terms. Evidence lies in the becoming evident, the mounting pressure of tangible evidence, evidence from under the subject's own skin, the presence of evidence to which its epidermis bears witness. Sensation, taste, palpability, tangibility: these are perceptible signs of subjective immediacy, the subject's immediacy to itself. Their signifying power and their signification lies in the way they present themselves by bringing to an end preoccupation and indisposability of self-love. In the negative, meaning can be read in the ruptured tissue of objectivity as though interpreting through the entrails of a sacrificial beast. Affirmatively, meaning resides in the recurrence of correspondence that takes place when the subject again becomes co-respondent, unveils itself to one able to speak and be spoken to. Or more specifically, disclosure is the atmosphere of one able to name and be named, to say the arche name *I* and to bear reponsibility for the naming of myself and the things *I* name.

Voice of essence, whose vocality differs markedly from that of objectivity, correspondence speaks from the midst of the self-hiding of consciousness. In order to prevent the unanticipated, the grasping of memory takes an interior posture in the body that is doubled over its middle, clenched, and unyielding. Since this frozen attitude constricts fluidity to the degree that even time runs off and sinks down, temporal quickening, the time of phenomenal birthing, is precluded. In its tyranny of equality, consciousness is particularly apprehensive about disruptive anarchy, the unruly rule of no thing over no other thing. In its secret self-enclosure, armed with multiple names for singularity, consciousness must be fractured if it is to speak in the voice of difference. The other breaks through to end the endless forgetting, and memory of correspondence is reborn. Spoken in the middle voice that is reserved for prayer, prophecy, and poetry, correspondence, the *sponde* [Greek], a drink offering, is the libation over disclosure, a mutual libating to what is higher, from disclosed to recipient, from the other to the one. In the speaking of essence—correspondence—meaning is conveyed through the reciprocity of prayer. As the essence of "herb or stone" unveils itself to a percipient consciousness, that consciousness turns toward the essential; and the reciprocal offering, the turning of each toward the other, evokes the response of that which is higher, in the form of a glad marking of the correspondence. Thus does correspondence lead to correspondence, lower correspondence to higher, all within Proclus's perception of sympathy.

I can speak my essential name, the arche name *I*, only in the presence of the other. Since meaning, in its exalted repetition of the voice of essence, arises from this naming, designation and signification in general are refutations of solipsism. The wrenching of essence from its hiding place is necessarily on behalf of the other. Discovery itself works through disruptive force that differentiates this plant from that; the *sym-pathein* of percipience is already sensitive to what is specifically other; the search is moved by a beneficence to share the fruits to alleviate the other's suffering. In co-responding, consciousness has left behind a self-imposed isolation and is somatically attuned to a region in which the essence of its subjectivity appears. Listening, it listens to the hyletic flow for the sounding of *I* that subvocally accompanies a manifestation of the essential. In such a position, it is on call for the solicitation of meaning, of the mysterious interchange that takes place between essence and essence.

9

SYMPATHY AND THE PLIGHT OF THE SELF

"No essence but essence." Since essence is the essential, we might be misled into thinking it is everywhere the same and thus be led back to a polity of equals that equally share in a common property. Such seems to be Proclus's notion. Because essence belongs to and *is* essentially subjectivity, it cannot be a property among properties that somehow takes hold of the being of a subject, nor can it belong to the predicate, the accusative nominative, to trail a faceless subject slinking from an evil eye. Far from being a stasis or hypostasis, essence is a *dynamis* that operates through an appropriative gesture. Essence has to do with letting-be-its-own, a letting be my own in the face of what is different. A thought, feeling, or sensation, when let be mine in the face of the other than mine, discloses an essential aspect of my subjectivity. *That I am.* If meaning is an annunciation of the advent of essence—this molding of matter into the ownmost of its being subject—then Heidegger's view concerning "*Ereignis*: the event of Appropriation" is essentialism.[1] If meaning is the herald of essence, then Heidegger propounds an essentialism for a theory of meaning. Since Ereignis is a deliverance of both time and Being over to what is their own, it implies a double coincidence, of the subject onto its own presence as well as its own openness. Ceasing its alienation from itself, owning itself, subjectivity lets itself become what it essentially is. It comes into contact with a current of meaningfulness and, in a gesture of appropriation, makes that meaning its own.

The binding together of essence, meaning, and difference into a supercompressed nucleus accounts for their explosive expansion throughout the universe of discourse. The initiatory spark that transforms the eternally fixed empyrean into a perpetually agitated cosmos is disruption. Disruption, coeval with God, a Titan before Olympus dreamed of power, spews its anarchaic creation across the expanse of subjectivity, and for the first time the arche name *I* is voiced. The firmament of consciousness, self-sustaining through the action of self-love, crumbles, and at the edges, uniquenesses that belong uniquely to the subject appear. With the appearance of difference, contemporaneous with the alteration of consciousness, consciousness is moved by the other and acquires movement. With the fragmentation of the same, an appropriative gesture, the embrace of ownness, the eo ipso, lets mine be mine. Far from being an impersonal lexical entry, *this*—that which I have let be my own—has meaning for me. As the prefiguration of essence becomes embodiment of the essential, voice is given a body. The arche name becomes incarnate and whatever it utters is meaningful. In breath, the pulse of blood, and the synaptic firing of the nerves, subjectivity comes to life . . . until movement and voice subside, and I, ceasing to coincide with myself in the present, become again a player in a story that I tell myself.

Essence, though everywhere essence, does not show itself in the letting-be-its-own any more than does the source of vibration in an acoustical experience. The appropriative gesture is the secret of essence, a work taken on as an initiatory promise and hence an ongoing ordeal, endless and without relief. Because of its avowal, essence is initiatory in the sense that subjectivity's encounter with essence initiates it into its own secret vow, the immemorable memory, the amnestic. Since to maintain the secret doctrine as secret would be to render being unapproachable and exclusive, even to coworkers, essence leaves marks of its work. The secret doctrine is an open secret, or in the trope of the artist, as Paracelus suggests, essence does not withdraw behind its vow without a trace but adds a signature to each appropriated uniqueness.

> Nature is the sculptor: she endows everything with the form which is also the essence, and thus the form reveals the essence. . . . There is nothing that nature has not signed in such a way that man may discover its essence.[2]

The signing of essence is, therefore, an act of sympathy. If it lacked feeling for the manifest, essence would remain unmanifest, behind its veil, mutely and interiorly at work. Sympathy, by contrast, motivates the force of appropriation toward designation of meaning. In allowing a portion of the ownness to be drawn by attraction to the exterior, sympathy creates signification. The totality of signs, their adjuncts and cognates, make up a universe of discourse bound and bounded by sympathy, a language articulated and made articulate by compassion.

The language of essence—the essential of discourse—is that which is designated for signification by sympathy. Sympathy turns essence outward, toward accident, contingency, and appearance, away from secret avowal of imperceptibility. Before its inevitable withdrawal, essence leaves a signature of its presence so as to indicate the road to discovery. Since in the totality of signs none is turned inward, each is turned to face the other, each faces the other because that is the direction of sympathy. No sign that essence has signed is self-absorbed, insular, isolated, solitudinous, and therefore unavailable for articulating with any other sign. Since each is a mark left by the gesture that gathers unto its own that which is its own, no one may be substituted for another. Inequality that is the secret work of essence is preserved by the action of sympathy. Since all signs are, as it were, ringed round the great round of designation, face to face, each co-responds with the other. Since there is no indifference, each sign picks up the speech of the other, amplifying it in such as way as to make the speaking its own. The designated meaning of one sign is picked up and carried on in the concert of the other until it echoes within a symphony of otherness.

This irrepressible speaking back and forth and up and down the great chain of being—the veritable babble of created creatures—results from the reticence and sympathy of essence. Though the lines of correspondences, horizontal and vertical, of a Paracelsus emerge gradually from inaudibility, the system they form does not compromise the singularity or dilute the identity of each conversant. Without striving for a synthesis, the discourse is not dialectical and does not gather into a larger unity that which is already whole unto itself. The totality of signs has a double function that we should remember. Poetically, it is a eulogy on the goodness of essence since value rather than necessity prompted its embrace of sympathy that gives us signs.

Inversely, to read a sign and uncover the essence of a thing is to know its specific goodness, for example, "the thistle, do not its leaves prickle like needles? Thanks to this sign, the art of magic discovered that there is no better herb against internal prickling."[3] To read is to know that the meaning of the sign "prickly leaves" has to do with a regenerative effect thistle has on the human body. It is to know that meaning denotes a unique quality of thistle insofar as it acts on subjectivity and insofar as it is discoverable by co-respondence.

"Only essence knows essence." However powerful a knowledge the system of signs yields in medicine and in the earth and human sciences, the exterior speech of essence reserves a special role for subjectivity. The speciality consists in how the human essence, in being called forth in the appropriative gesture, lets its own be its own and thereby discloses the meaning of meaning. Subjectivity reveals the goodness of essence as it reads the signs indicative of essence and comes to be co-respondent to the essence of a thing. Since the reading is a double action whereby the subject unveils its own to itself simultaneous to its unveiling the thing's own to the thing, subjectivity stands naked in its essential knowledge. The special work of human subjectivity is to disclose the work of essence, and thus to initiate itself into essence's secret initiatory vow.

That vow, the turning toward manifestation through sympathy, is echoed in subjectivity's disclosure of the sign. Although things bear their designations from the time of creation, signification remains clandestine and inward until consciousness speaks the speech. Although things are ringed around, facing toward each other, essence is unable to manifest sympathetically until its designations are consciously articulated, that is, until signs are deciphered and virtue, goodness, and meaning made known. Human language is not so much the fulfillment of essential signification as its salvation, for without the intervention of subjectivity, the initiatory vow would be a lie, and sympathy a sham. When consciousness is brought into language with the openness of subjectivity, sympathy is realized as sympathy. When the designations that have waited mutely since before eternity are granted voice, human voice becomes the voice of the subject who officiates over its own initiation—who initiates itself into its own.

Becoming co-respondent, subjectivity returns its essential core to the active role of steward of sympathy. A preexisting language, gift of essence, revives through percipience, as an archeologist returns an ancient script to life by deciphering it. The language, the text of inner signs and outward marks, moreover, has a double meaning since its deciphering reveals as much about the reader as the read. The irradicable ambiguity of designation imples that through the microcosm, the macrocosm is made manifest, and vice versa. Given the hermetic principle of "as above, so below," sympathy is none other than the hieratic guide to the unmanifest. As Paracelsus declares, "there is nothing in man that is not marked in his exterior, so that by the exterior one may discover what is in the individual who bears the sign."[4] Since percipience is a surface that faces both directions and like a Moebius strip has a single face, it is fully capable of the task of decoding the ambiguity. Its power may be attributed to a new agent, one hitherto unengaged by consciousness. When consciousness recurs in a somatic logos, the inner or subtle body bears the text of correspondence. It is that on which signs appear to be inscribed, and so, to read the inscription is to read its own—to know itself essentially. Since, conversely, the system of signs reveals the presence of the subtle body, it too must be the "hidden treasure" whose spot is marked by special traits. The discernment that the prickly leaves of the thistle are a sign attests to the subtle body's presence since "only essence knows essence." The subtle body's presence, therefore, gives testimony to the essence of subjectivity. The tragedy of the subtle body, from Descartes onward to our time, lies in the fact that its neglect is eo ipso neglect of essence.

The disclosure of essence, its secret text and vow, does not exhaust subjectivity, and the view that it does—essentialism—traps the subject in the universe of discourse. A cursive and discursive entity, subjectivity is caught up in signification and lives with its ears pricked for new meaning. It becomes a collector of texts, an archeologist expert at a kind of hermeneutics, a contributor to the lexicon, a patron of the arts of designation. Developing a sensitivity to the inner constitution of things, subjectivity spreads out its discoveries in a tissue of correspondences and imagines itself a cartographer or scribe. That essence itself disrupts the sleep of being and before subsiding vows to bring forth knowledge of its own is forgotten by subjectivity. The memory that disrupts forgetfulness—even the lethe that is fascination for meaning—brings the subject face to face with the other that memory springs from before the time of essence's promise, from before the time of time. Disruption shows the limits of essentialism, of the meaning of meaning, because in it resounds the ethical. Where the symmetry between microcosm and macrocosm shatters, there the fact of obligation reappears. That the obligation to support the other preexists meaning, intentionality, and consciousness breaks the harmony of correspondences like a cry for help in the dark of night. That the obligation is not my own, that I do not come to it by an appropriative gesture, that it waits for me like a skin to fit into, puts an end to ontology and hermeneutics. The ethical is where I come in, not by my own doing, but because I am done to. Where subjectivity ends its affair with meaning, it begins its responsible work: that by contact and exchange with the other, the continual creation of creation be continually sustained.

Infatuation may be a deficiency of sympathy or its theme. Sympathy may inevitably fall in love with the servants of its compassion, or it may serve them with the passion for the *fatuus*, the absurd. In either case, the subject's infatuation with meaning—the child of sympathy—and with the meaning of meaning—the semiotics of self—amounts to a rapture. The imperialism of meaning is a state of lethe in which an aspect of essence's secret vow is ignored. The sympathy of openness that spawns the totality of signs aspires eternally to know the principle that eternally initiates it. At the same act that it yields the universe of discourse, the essence that is everywhere, essence yearns to be *beyond* its revealed being and once more be a servant of that from which it received orders. It yearns to be done with its ontological gesture and once more face to face with that which takes precedence, the ethical commitment that cleaved essence from being and imbued it with sympathy. It aspires to know the preoriginal disruptive force, directly, without modifications or adornments, in its dwelling beyond being. Its yearning and aspiration are its suffering, the essential suffering of creation, because of their impossibility. Disruption, the unmanifest, that which is *not*, the *theos agnostus*, cannot be met because it is that which breaks up every meeting.

When the subject's rapture with meaning comes to a stop and the pathos of sympathy—of the signs ringed round face to face in order to speak of essence to essence—subjectivity recalls its ethical incompleteness. Inasmuch as this recollection differs from that of the ontological deficiency, about which Marcel expresses concern, it does not have to do with the suffering to mean or to be. It is not about becoming my own, following the secret trail to essence, or recapturing the lost meaning of things and self. That such suffering is for the reembodiment of goodness is as undeniable as the fact that it is not yet ethical suffering. Disrupting the suffering to mean or to be, the ethical centers on the other and his/her suffering. It concerns initiation into the fact of obligation, into the fact that the other's pain needs to be owned as my own. While an appropriative gesture, this owning has less to do with ontology or semiotics than with the tortured cry of my fellow creature. The other's call to help lift his/her burden, to show that I am *I*, the arche name, by meeting the face of rage, pity, fear, or greed with an acknowledgment of the higher. In the ethical, I leave behind my adoration of the sign-signified relation, and, embracing what takes precedence, reveal the pupose of our being together: to transform his/her suffering into the dignity of an ethical work.

10

"BECOMING SIMILAR"

Laws of correspondence that bring together signature and secret essence presuppose a co-respondent subject. Microcosm reveals what being conceals. Thus, in the totality of signs, subjectivity is not in a position of privilege but of subposition, is not a whole greater than the totality but a lesser, subordinate whole that is under orders. The subject as a sign speaks and responds as one among the many signs, and at the same time is percipient of the meanings. Though a meaning among meanings, subjectivity involves the meaning of meaning, wherein lies its special and specific place. It alone among the many signs is capable of taking on essence's vow of sympathy for its own, of being like essence but for the subject itself. This appropriative gesture, letting its own be its own, allows subjectivity to appropriate meaning for its own, that is, to take hold of the meaning of meaning.

"Like is known by like," writes Aristotle, citing Empedocles as saying, "With earth do we see earth, with water water, with air bright air, with fire consuming fire; with Love do we see Love, Strife with dread Strife."[1] Correspondence is inscribed in the text of likeness. Since reading signs implies being correspondent to them, subjectivity becomes essencelike, resembling most nearly that which in it corresponds to the essential. To the thought of essentialism, consciousness abdicates the power to constitute itself, and with the openness of the appropriative gesture, becomes a presence in the world. All depends on an act of abnegation when emperor is suddenly enlightened and drops the reins of imperialism. Since the view implies that altered consciousness is a matter of volition and intention, essentialism is motivated by self-will and autonomous self-legislation. Kant is closer to the truth when he places spontaneity, the absence of self-caused causes, at helm of a freely altered consciousness. Contrary to essentialism, quite out of the blue, disruption strikes and the for-itself lurches into contact with the other. A world-shattering event, it annihilates the realm of substitution and representation, leaving an empty hall where once the mirrors stood. Its self-absorption ended, consciousness quickens and comes to a percipient awareness of the matrix of meaning. Thus beginning its kinship to likeness, it grows more knowing of its own meaning.

Out of a sympathy for the manifest, essence divulges its presence through signs that are *like* it. Though their likeness is not representational (as a photograph is to a scene), signs furnish an image of the particular essence. "Behold the *Satyrion* root," writes Paracelsus. "Is it not formed like the male privy parts? . . . it can restore a man's virility and passion."[2] Although hidden lines of convergence remain to be found, to have perceived what the form is *like* is already to have performed the major part of deciphering. A consciousness able to form an image of likeness is one that, having been struck by an appearance, is on the verge of alteration. If we take Eckhart's words as guide, that "outside of likeness, one cannot speak of an image," then such a consciousness has acquired an active imagination.[3] Having little in common with Kant's device of a productive imagination, a synthesizing force relegated to the transcendental shadows, active imagination derives the sympathetic sensibility from the somatic logos. Originating with the hyletic flow's power to be struck by ambient impressions that emanate from the essence of things, it is fruit of a consciousness vulnerable to alteration. When an emanation strikes the imagination and likeness is impressed, consciousness is on its way to knowing the works of sympathy. Such knowledge differs from that of self-constituting perception which utilizes the spatio-temporal framework, which visually sees the *Satyrion* root in a certain shape, texture, color, and solidity. When perceiving *Satyrion* as *like* the male genitalia, imagination has a primary perception of likeness and a secondary one of the individual essences that are related by correspondence.

Active imagination, far from being an intellectual process, is the work of percipience. Becoming *like*, the somatic logos remembers the secret vow of essence and "inhabits" the body of sympathy. Not a literal inhabitation, but an incarnation of essential intelligibility and sensitivity, the sympathetic body carries out the initiatic task of disclosing being and making known the hidden core of things. Through the trope of similitude, percipience attempts to dispel a literal reduction to sameness. The image active in active imagination is the co-respondent's contribution to the conversation that sympathy evokes from essence. If it contains pieces or parts of the particular essence from which it emanates, the contents are like those of a response to a sentence that contains phrases or fragments of the original. They are not literally the same because contact implies one meeting the other and being transformed through the exchange with the other. Early theories of perception such as Empedocles's suffer from a confusion of active with passive, sameness with similarity, and gross body with subtle body. To say that "perception arises when something fits into the passages of any of the senses" is to fall into a literal-mindedness that depicts emissaries of equality who bear messages from one to the other.[4] It is to overlook the crux of communication which occurs when the exterior evokes recollection from "within the things themselves."

The degradation of likeness from the auspicious power of perceiving correspondence to the myoptic vision that mars modern idealist theories stems from the denial of disruption. Descartes's calumny heaped upon the senses comes from the corroding effect of likeness made feeble. When he complains that "there is no likeness at all . . . between the sensation of an object that gives me pain and the experience (*cognitationem*) of sadness that arises from the sensation,"[5] the sympathetic source has already been betrayed, and likeness reduced to equality. Perception has ceased to be in correspondence with the secret oath of essence, and instead gathers intelligence for the coming hegemony of consciousness. Its function is to forearm consciousness against the assault of difference and its effects so pernicious to self-legislation. Inasmuch as likeness is contingent on difference (or else it could not relate different corresponds), it is annihilated, reduced to a substitute for sameness, synonomized, humiliated. A powerful, inhuman ignorance now passes for the knowledge of sympathy. Whereas before a necessary and insoluble bond linked suffering and its cause, a deep, unshakeable correspondence that gave testimony to the correctness of a discourse, now the connection is haphazard, subject to dispute, of questionable concern, and proof of the infallibility of sensation. Consciousness can no longer rely on felt sadness to know the other's suffering since likeness equals sameness and one's consciousness is not the same as the other's. Since consciousness can no longer be altered in response to its anarchaic imperative and meet the other's need with pity, it remains isolated in its own terrible suffering—that it has ceased to be certain of anything but its self-certainty.

The ruination of imagination is its stultification. That it becomes merely a contemplative of "the likeness of picture of a body" means that the self-enclosing of signification protectively encircles consciousness.[6] Signs encrust the single face of the double percipient surface, and imagination, having become recombinant, has lost touch with the essential emanations of world and subject. Consciousness is fixed, docile, saturated with imagery, democratic. Philosophy is ready for a Locke.

To live in denial of the Aristotlean principle, like knows like, is to deny alteration. If, as Empedocles argues, eros alone sees eros and eris, eris, denial involves a clandestine annihilation of the disruptive element of subjectivity. Strife and anarchy, like seeds of a fiery memory, flare up without provocation, cause, reason, warning, putting on the habit of emotions, sensations, or insurrectionary thoughts, to reclaim the subject for spontaneity—Kantian freedom. When a forceful or subtle injection of difference into the play of an enfeebled imagination disintegrates the state of consciousness, consciousness per se can emerge. If the seed of memory, ever ready to burst to incandescence, is interred in uncombustibles, it cannot germinate action, and, perhaps, languishes away. "This spark," Eckhart writes, "is the higher part of the spirit; in it is located the image of the mind."[7] Since eris is higher than eros, since it predates eros—the created and manifest—by virtue of being uncreated and coeval with the principle of creation, the seed of disruption that threatens self-created consciousness incarnates the higher such as belongs to subjectivity. Since the disruptive spark—Eckhart's adaptation of the Aristotelean *nous*—is the immemorable memory of what takes precedence, it implies a displacement and destabilization of consciousness as well as a recentering of orbits around subjectivity. Consciousness's egocentrism gives way to a altrocentrism in which mind, reimaged and recontured, remembers its own subordination. At the same time, the seed no more belongs to the subject than the embryo does to the mother. Since it is a memory that cannot be gathered in by the appropriative gesture, cannot become the subject's own, it is forever wild, ungovernable, and under rule of higher laws. Although its action is felt on the level of subjectivity, its origin—like a terrifying angel's—lies above the origin of the subject.

That subjectivity contains an element not its own or of its own origination implies that the subject can never entirely coincide with himself/herself. Like Russell's set of all sets that do not belong to themselves, the closure of subjectivity is forever in logical contradiction. The conflict with logos is heighteneed by the fact that the subject is a set that contains a member that contains the set, for how else can an image of consciousness be located in the disruptive seed? The projects to uncover the logical limits of consciousness, the transcendental bounds of the self-constituting self, or the possibilizing horizons of the for-itself operate in ignorance of this alogical germ that inheres in subjectivity. Incompleteness, noncongruence, and misappropriateness color subjectivity so radically that only obsession can negate them. Revising a theme of Kierkegaard, we can say that the self is a relation that does not relate to itself, or that in the relation that does not, because it includes an element not its own. Like a gold nugget in a vein of quartz, the inclusiveness of self is such that it includes that which is nonself—the other.

Beyond reason, meaning, and the totality of signs ringed round, the undying anarchaic ember answers to no thing, and from its source in the unmanifest, dictates to all. Through that dictation, in the voice of recurrent disruption, the autoproduction of consciousness quiets to a murmur and the speech of sympathy made audible. Beyond fulfilling the inner word of essence and disseminating its particles across creation, the cacophonous strains of disruption presents, in Eckhart's thought, an image of consciousness. Imaging is unsolicitated, unordained, and unthought. Though the image is not consciousness itself, it is *like* consciousness in that it co-responds to consciousness the way that consciousness is percipiently able to co-respond to the essence of things. Its inchoate unruliness does not negate its sympathetic penchant to correspond. Just as consciousness's communication with things depends on its embodiment, so too the image's communication is contingent on its incarnation, for only through the vehicle of a higher body or somatic logos does percipience work. The kernel of its speech, furthermore, is to communicate the likeness to consciousness itself, just as consciousness communicates the likenesses of things across creation. The image's presence, therefore, implies a level of speaking within the influence of sympathy but beyond essence and the totality of signs. The speaking that is not the speech *of* but *to* consciousness concerns the ethical. Sympathy speaks not only in the indicative but also the imperative.

The seed that spontaneously combusts, incinerating the for-itself contains a likeness that differs from the essence of consciousness—or else there would be perfect coincidence between image and essence. The difference that can never be unmade, the uneradicable gap, is, however, not empty but full of speech. Even when memory fades and the immemorable is forgotten, the residue of speaking remains, persistently obtruding in designation and even in substitution by synonomy, summoning sensitivity as well as reflection. The imperative voice conveys a command, the command that consciousness become more like the disruptive likeness of itself. The contradiction that the form states, "Become similar to a likeness you are not and which is other than you," is the contradiction definitive of the ethical. The embodiment of an image of consciousness whose origination is beyond essence is the baring of conscience within subjectivity. It is the search for a way of transforming the self through a sympathetic heart.

The similitude consciousness enjoys to the world differs from that it bears to the seed as indicative does to imperative or as nominative does to accusative. Through the first similitude, consciousness becomes ontological, its essential self, knowledge, a being among beings whose role is to disclose being. Through the second similitude, consciousness becomes deontological, subordinate, responsible, a human among humans whose task is to assist the other. The abrupt shift in voice and case (in Kant's phrase) from the starry heavens to the moral law is a sacrifice in the consolation of knowledge. The sacrificial prize of designation, won at no small cost, is an orientation, a schooling. "In the stars," Paracelsus writes,

> all skills are arts, all crafts are hidden, and also all wisdom, all reason, as well as foolishness and what belongs to it. . . . The stars are our school in which everything must be learned.[8]

This inner bracketing of the natural attitude breaks the spell cast by the ageless murmuring of nature. When knowledge of signs and intelligible forms fragments and the still background to meaning assumes command, the obedience of consciousness takes precedence. The task of acquiring similitude to that which has no similar waits like a skin, like a nakedness. The tear-streaked face of the other—the one I am not, the one whose suffering I ought to put on—disrupts the search for meaning with the obligation of love. To turn from the blood-stained ground and back to my knowledge is to ignore the fact that I am in the accusative, under accusation, accused of denying similarity, until I answer. To remain silent when the skin crawls with the other's nausea is to be counted out, to be condemned by indifference.

That like knows like puts the question of what the seed of disruption is *like*. Although eris knows eris, to what is Strife itself similar? Since the sympathetic expression of disruptive force is difference, though Strife is like no other, likeness is its fruit. Without differentiation, discord, and destabilization, union would be impossible. Strife, the disintegrative current that originates beyond essence, sets the constellation of uniquenesses awhirling in the temporality of presence, addressing one another in a concert of designation. Roused from the sleep of being, the ontological slumber that is its natural condition, consciousness speaks of speaking, and learning from the school of things, seeks their integral and its own. Recovering its primal voice, consciousness speaks the arche name, *I*. The other names speak back. In that action, Love, whose likeness is sympathetically repeated in each thing, is sought. Only eris, the incomparable, lacks designation and remains apart from the concert of being. As unmanifest as unmanifest divinity, it is no God unless the cause of creation be internal to the Godhead. As timeless as the divine Word, its endless disruption of eternal peace is reason enough for the continuous disclosure of substance, mode, and essence.

11

NONDISCLOSURE

To disclosure corresponds essence, the world of being, signification, and the stirring of sympathy—that secret promise to disavow the unmanifest and to become manifest. In modern times since Descartes, ontology has defined the extent of philosophy since designation records the act of standing forth, taking a step forward from a uniform, undifferentiated, indifferent background. Kant's rejection of intelligible objects, the clearest statement of the limiting factor of disclosure, precludes the nonphenomenal, the nontransparent, the indemonstrable, and the unknown from meaning and discourse. This idealist tendency—not the idealism that Kant refutes (that "the existence of objects in space outside us [is] either merely doubtful and indemonstrable or to be false and impossible") but that which champions the concept as standard of signification—focuses attention on becoming manifest.[1] Since this act, as the root speaks, is a striking forth by the hand—violence and volition—philosophy has centered its concern on a particular disruption, namely, the intentional, self-willed, self-originating impulse to unveil the yet veiled reality, to dwell openly in the openness of pure presence. That which involves no disclosure is thereby excluded from the sanctified circle of inquiry. The very idea of nondisclosure implies a concealment, a lie, a feigning of truth, cowardice, closure, an inquiry into meaning blocked before the first step can be taken.

Disclosure, the forcible tearing the terms of a promise from essence's breast, the demanding of compliance and culpability from essence, encircles philosophy like a fascination. The trope of charm, exclaimed by Alcibiades as climax to philosophy's dialectic of love, seems appropriate to the spell of discourse and essence: "I am smitten with a kind of sacred rage, worse than any Corybant, and my heart jumps into my mouth and the tears start into my eyes."[2] "Sacred rage," a description that is true to the violence of ontology—subjectivity's demand on essence to stand forth—clearly states the theological, transcendental proclivities of being. It also draws forth another fundamental connection, that between thought and anger. The Greek *mentis* and *menos* both mean "wrath" or "anger" while the second is related to the Latin *mens*, meaning besides "anger," "thinking, intention, deliberation, imagination." Discourse or directed thought takes its direction toward disclosure, phenomena, objects, and running off time from the impetus of anger . . . and away from opacity, noumena, immediacy, disruption. Could we say that discourse, that monument to human awareness, is disruption made undisruptive, stilled, quiescent? Anger, one's reaction, according to Descartes, to harm to self, is an emotion especially characteristic of ego.[3] That thought, consciousness's process toward the intentional object, toward that which it would make good essence's vow to disclose itself, is driven by force of rage makes it ironic that thought is a principle of disclosure—since rage is opaque to itself. But then, dissembling, feigning, tricking, saying the opposite of what is meant—irony itself—is one of the chief tropes of inquiry. Without ironic incongruity, the noncoincidence of subjectivity with itself, consciousness would be limited by rectitude, rigor, and an unmitigated literalmindedness in its task of disclosure.

Signification and the signs of essence ringed round, all of subjectivity's valiant effort to make good on essence's vow, expands to fill the entire text of philosophy. Sacred rage that rejects the profanity of cowardice—the way the coward abets the concealment of being—carries a banner difficult to ignore. The disruption by discursive thought of low-level autoproduction of consciousness becomes the standard by which disclosure is measured. Unless the mental effort to think *through* is present, inferior processes of self-constitution prevail—or so goes Descartes's great temptation to use thought whose origin is rage as the basis of identity. Intellectual knowledge swells to become knowledge per se, within which one sign can be substituted for another without loss and beyond which is only the abiding illusion of a transcendental substitute. Even Kant's idea of a transcendental illusion that "does not cease even after it has been detected" prompts the further delusion that beyond the concept, essential meaning, and the knowing subject lies a something that, for dint of a slightly greater effort, would be brought into the fold of meaning—a proto-concept or substratum of a sign.[4]

The denigration of the nondisclosed, or even the nondisclosable, is part of Heidegger's thought of "Being in the sense of the presencing and allowing-to-presence that are there in destiny."[5] That which wrenches or lets be wrenched from the ontological bedrock is granted the priority of predestination and prefigurement. Although unpredicatable, Ereignis, the meaningful event, that which makes it one's own, is prefigured in the constitution of subjectivity, the way remembrance prefigures certain occurrences like death. Being lights up in the open, presence dispels the spell of lethe, the forgetful, and the totality of signs radiates so that temporality itself joins in the event. For Heidegger, the resistant, dogged absence of the unmanifest must itself be overcome until a sanctification occurs since

> what is unconcealed is what has entered into the rest of pure appearing and outward appearance. What is unconcealed is what is thus sheltered.[6]

In a light holy and hushed, an inner reverence does a vigil for augurs and portents. In an act of godliness, the ego has been dismissed in order to assume the role of shepherd of being. Yet in wresting appearance from concealment lies a concealed disruption, a striving, an effort, a conatus, that lacks the transparency of the manifest, a restlessness in the face of absence. The disruption that ushers manifestation into the shelter of discourse, furthermore, can never be unconcealed, presented in repose, signified definitively, or said to be. Ancestor to the origin of the impulse of disclosure, it defies the holy like an excommunicant or a heretic and makes eccentric the circle of being. It—that one—absent, nonbeing, unrevealed, is that which ontology avoids when it avoids walking in its own skin.

Ontology is shelter and dwelling. Enclave, safe house, refuge, haven, harbor, asylum, ontology preserves signification, in counterpoint to the preservation of concealment that preserves the hidden and unmeaning. Meaning is thereby protected from the indefinable and unanticipated—the disruptive. When meaning ceases to be devoured by the wolves of concealment, memory is reinforced. Not memory of the immemorable (which is disruptive) but of the retainable, such memory gathers meaning around it against future assailants. When disclosure and essence define the exclusive province of philosophy, concealment is a mode of or subordinate to unconcealment. It would be unveiled but for. . . . The force of revelation, assumed to be passive or active, is predestined to triumph over absence like light over darkness because of its higher origin. Since revelation itself derives its stunning power from disruption, disruption merely putting on that suit of clothes, ontology's shelter for appearance begins to appear self-protective. What about the nondisclosed that lets the unmanifest remain unmanifest, that does not seek out the signs in order to trace essence back to its lair? That nontransparency seeks no ontological shelter but visits the touch of touch, the tactility of contact, like a wild one, as Enkidu before he was tamed. In the sensation of sense arises a vulnerability or assailability alien to disclosure, around which disclosure closes like a fist around the wind. The restlessness of pure unappearing, the black hole whose gravity sucks appearance from being, it is that which in contact, in the-one-with-the-other, cannot be unveiled or thought because it disrupts both veil and unveiling, thought and unthought. Since the voice is imperative, disruption commands without analogy, parable, metaphor, likeness, or trope. The command is to the heart of the matter and what matters is obedience. Not to obey the command that breaks the ontological trance is to commit suicide, to walk out of one's skin, to sell one's lover for a slave. Disobedience, living with one's death warrant signed, is giving over again to indifference everything wrested from essence and ending up a traitor among one's own people. The disruption that originates higher than being recollects the inescapable: that before ontology is deontology and that, regardless of disclosure, one is obligated by the fact of obligation.

The ethical does not transcend sympathy in order to nullify it, as though looking for grounds for retracting a promise, but treats it more totally, more sympathetically, than does disclosure, Dasein, and essentialism. Obligation derives from an aspiration to encompass not only being but the beyond-being, not only presence and coming-to-presence but the never-to-come-to-presence. Since it yearns to serve the unmanifest of the unmanifest and cannot, sympathy is intrinsically with-pathos, a sadness that the face of the other evokes, a sorrow never to be erased by joy. The other's suffering, apparent or hidden beneath a veil of good cheer, calls me to an absence in myself that I suffer, that I cannot atone for—an incompleteness that being cannot complete. Furthermore, enjoyment is not negated by sadness nor sadness by enjoyment, but since both are twin faces through which the hidden expresses without surrendering its concealment, neither is changed by that expression. Sadness and enjoyment fail to enter fully into disclosure because they are modes of sensitivity, are of the body and, as Spinoza notices, are useful to the extent that they increase or decrease the body's perception.[7] The failure to enter fully into the charmed circle of unveiling is, moreover, no deficiency in sadness (or joy), no evidence of being's withdrawal, no proof that Western metaphysics has gone astray, no presumption of sin (Marcel). Sadness's nondisclosure is its remaining true to sympathy, its allegiance to the unveiled, its courageous contact with the disruptive other. After all the saying is said, a part of sadness remains sad, without recognition, without the possibility of recognition.

A somatic event, an event of percipience or sensitivity such as desire, pleasure, or aversion, contains an aspect that is pure impulse or striving, a conatus. Inasmuch as it discloses itself only to the extent that it lends force and vivacity to immediacy, the remainder—a subtraction that can never be tallied—is veiled. The veiling is not of a "something I know not what," Locke's presumption of a substantive failure of ontology, nor does it pertain to a matter, as Hume believes, for physiologists, natural science, and a metaphysics of sameness. The veiling is itself a vulnerability that cannot show itself because to show would be to disrupt the vulnerability, to destroy it, to disturb it, to alter its nonbeing, to modify it through revelation, to superimpose meaning onto its unmeaning. Inasmuch as vulnerability remains a summons without a summoner, an imperative without a commander, it issues from a hiding place without giving itself away. Its commandment has nothing to do with the signification of being or the recognition of essence—acts of a free, self-legislating consciousness—but with obedience. The command of vulnerability is as absolute as the identity of the commander is absolutely undisclosed. From an undisclosed origin, from before time and space originate, one is anachronistically commanded to answer for the other's vulnerability, to bind his/her wounds with the shirt off one's own back. The other's vulnerability—my own in the other's skin, his/her own in mine—touches an undisclosed place in my heart, a gentle touch of condolence at the elbow, and I respond absolutely, in need of no unveiling whatsoever. I respond because the command awaited my birth, my human form, since the command awaited the birth of humanity before the conception of a human species.

When the subtle body is in contact with the other, the wordless commandment of vulnerability resounds. Sensitivity, striving, and the conative, gather as advent to a disruption of being. Ontology is disrupted by deontology, signification by obligation, knowledge by blankness, freedom by subordination. Sympathy's unfulfillment that yearns to heal the wounded other disrupts its satisfaction with being, the plentitude, the plenum. Sympathy in contradiction with itself, strife against love, speaks of how a disruption to what already is established by disruption sounds the note of ethics. In self-conflict, the trope of sadness fits because the face of sadness turns away, becomes reticent, conceals its tears, hides its suffering from the other—even though sadness never concerns only the one who is sad, when one is alone licking one's wounds, since it involves a drawing the curtain in front of the face of the other. The openness of ethics, moreover, is different from the pastoral openness of essentialism. The openness of ethics is not like a door open in welcome or a field in readiness, but like the openness of a wound that does not heal. It is the openness of skin being open, of abrasion and incision, of inflammation that festers, of pain and injury, of invasion. The openness of ethics, against which there is no indemnity, invades the autonomous self, diminishing freedom, disrupting self-legislation.

Vulnerability, the smarting of the subtle body, is sensed in immediacy and erased in reflection. That to which sensitivity is vulnerable, the dative of vulnerability, is influence of the other. The other's claims for assistance assail one's self-possession, breach the gap, and assume unquestioned precedence. Heeded or not, they break the linear directedness of self-possession, forcing self-recovery or redirection toward a new goal, end, or object after the hiatus. In the interval itself comes the influx of commandment to stand before consciousness like a cripple, a beggar, a refugee, permitting no escape from its open palm. In that interval, one is victim, either to the absolute need of the other's running sores or to one's own refusal. Victimized by disruption, one feels one can do no other than duty—one feels unconditionality—and touches the other at the elbow, helps the other into one's own house, holds the other close to one's breast.

Since through contact, through the one-touching-the-other, the unmanifest is not unveiled and let be but continues to disturb the peace of being with imperatives, exchange does not occur in sleep. Exchange is not the gesture of appropriation, the gentleness of making that which one owns one's own, in the composure of one's being. Exchange makes the other's own mine, and in making his/her suffering my own, requires the total passivity and wakenness of a patient. Because at the same time I give succor to the other, I receive his/her pain, poverty, worthlessness, debility, because part of me goes to the other in return for part of him/her, I accept difference. I accept to trade places with the other, to take up the other's homelessness when offering him/her my own, to feel the other's hopelessness when giving over my hope. I eat off his/her plate and feed him from mine. The cost of exchange, accepting a lesser good in exchange of a greater, summons a wakefulness as little else can. Bearing the cost, being answerable to the obligation, one awakens to an awakening that predates pain, decrepitude, and refusal, an awakening that disrupts the patience of pain with the activism of service. Athough it is sacrifice, exchange involves no loss but in fact profits the initiator, arousing the force of a memory not attainable in any other way. The apex of vulnerability gives proof of the Socratic principle that suffering is a greater good than causing suffering.

Nondisclosure, sympathy of sympathies, and the commandment that does not reveal its source: these engender a susceptibility that is uniquely ethical. A disruption from higher than the disruption of ontology, ethics commands all and everything, yet its dismissal costs nothing—one even sleeps more soundly from it! An insomnia, a terror of arousal, a memory that jams into place with the panic of having been forgotten: the Damoclean sword that one who lives ethically lives under. Which is to say that one lives momentarily out of the retentive current, in explosive timeless time, until the next moment. To accept more the task of the other, the disruptive difference is to speak of praxis, of which I will speak below. For now, the ethical must be admitted as episodic, an intervention in automaticity, a note that sympathetically sounds in proximate sensitivities, a sporadic hunger to face an origination alien to one's own origin.

IV

SUMMONS

ARGUMENT

Disruption commands categorically, not through discourse (that speaks only of temporal continuity) but through the soma. The dream of autonomy, being a law unto oneself, is broken. Consciousness is accused of not fulfilling its responsibility—to a law not of its own making that predates the inception of the autonomous subject. Consciousness is called back to a forgotten extention of its subjectivity that responds with obedience to a call to uplift the other's humanity. One's brother or sister, one's neighbor, a stranger on the street: to meet the other face to face breaks with a vengeance into one's project of accomplishing liberation and reminds one of prior obligations that always take precedence. This is the meaning of the imperative Kant explores. To respond to the ethical—the enigmatic, vague, and exceptional—is continual trial. In the ordeal are found the keys of initiation, the conscious and voluntary encounter with disruption on its own terms. Before the discovery, the conditions of authentic praxis need to be examined since, on the face of it, it is impracticeable to try to remember the immemorial. In the very impracticability, an expansion of subjectivity adequate to obedience lies to conscience.

12

INITIATION

Voice in the imperative mood disrupts categorically. After discovering it, Kant was unable to see how effectively imperative voicing puts to an end the self-legislating, decisive nature of the subject and without qualification subjects it to an unwilled, unprincipled obedience. Although the imperative mood contradicts autonomy as an anarchist contradicts democracy, Kant's belief that categoricality originates with the ethical subject blinds him to the disruption. Like a call from sleep, from a somnolent state, that conveys an urgent matter (a call from one's sick child), imperative voicing rouses an immediacy that does not require hermeneutics because it speaks to the blood. The alarm voiced in the imperative is nonoriginary, does not concern the origin of consciousness and subjectivity, and is there to fill the ears before the infant's first cry. The voice sounds itself as an accusation, in the accusative, as the *kategorein*, the voice that in public raises itself to point the finger at the accused. In it resound the charges that await one's first move, that one walks into—like an unknown identity—although a stranger in the land, and from which one can never be cleared. The imperative speaks to a condition earlier than nativity, a condition of indebtedness that obligates categorically, in the sense that the debt must be worked on, always and everywhere, and not for oneself, but for the other. Although the basic charge is Promethean, of theft, of making no effort to return what is not one's own, the imperative also charges ingratitude and unprofitability. Since subjectivity, the unprofitable servant, is self-aggrandizing and abrogates working for another, the imperative voice is an accusation and an upsurge that discloses a resistance and refusal without disclosing itself.

Since in its self-constitution, subjectivity makes its own laws and conditions, it is forever vulnerable to the unconditional. Unmade, raw, nonmanufactured, the unconditioned is the unconditionable, and in the way that it perforates the skin of the conditioned subject, like so many darts of accusation, is never in agreement and always at odds with the one. The unconditional dispenses with what consciousness has allotted itself, its categories and predicaments, and particularly with the transcendental unity of apperception, the "I think" that the subject is capable of subvocally uttering. Inasmuch as the transcendental unity gives credence to an identity, an essence, that abides nominally in the transspatial and transtemporal regions of the mind, it obviates what need, exigence, taste, or *Urfuhl* indicates—an unconditional accusation that one is indebted, the debit is owed the other, and the other has claim to own what one takes as one's own. Since the imperative abruptly breaks into signification and the circle of meaning with its categorical needs, the transcendental unity evaporates like a self-righteous smile in front of a broken victim of war, and with it, the gesture of appropriation that makes one's own what is one's own. The dissolution of the golden chain of essentialism, its enchantments and spells, and the power of correspondence that accompanies it, leaves one exposed before the unconditional, a body unnerved by raw elements. In the chill, the event Ereignis cannot move the heart whose compassion is already moved by the unsaid, unutterable suffering that is the other's pain, to which one is charged to take on as one's own. An understanding heart is that which surpasses the essence of essentialism.

Since the recurrent voicing of unconditionality breaks in upon the mute, unresponsive shell of the for-itself and takes it to task, the subject suffers, exposed in proximity. Whereas meaning is a measure of being—because once disclosed, the graspable sign becomes a standard of appearance for that genus of being—now exposure measures responsibility. Responsibility has as little to do with decision as it does with freedom, lawfulness, or origination. Responsibility is the unchosen as well as the being chosen, that which hits one in the face, weighs on the heart, pulls at the gut. It is the wall one walks into, not knowing it is there until it is too late. It is, as Kant says, having to do something without wanting to, being called to touch the other at the elbow in spite of oneself, saying "Yes" when one's heart is in one's mouth. If one opts for consequentialism and responsibility were a matter of choice, then the ethical would not be the disruptive knock on the door, spilling one out of bed from the midst of dreams, in order to let the persecuted stranger in. Then resistance and refusal themselves would not be armaments against disruption, and the soul itself would not be seared by its indebtedness.

The imperative is voiced and its mood resounds, wakening responsibility, competence, and inadequacy at once, and since courage is ethical comportment, anxiety is by its side. That which stirs is an initiative that does not go blank facing the blank face of the other, the other's incapacity and need, but which reaches out to help the other in. That the disruption that shakes the sheltering house of being is met means contact and exchange and signifies as no sign can signify the humanity of effort. Essential disguise rent into pieces, exposed to the indeclinable, subjectivity responds by transforming exposure into initiative. Faced with the acosmic power that lacks a beginning, the subject gathers matter for a beginning of his/her own. Since one's own beginning is not owned by a gesture of appropriation that has the cooperation of the realm of essence and the totality of signs, its meaning is different. It is the meaning of one who is powerless, without options, absent, and not understanding presence, who has to make a beginning—or die. The opposite of beginning to live an ethical life is, as Camus knows, suicide since it involves the embrace of self-importance plus complete ignorance. The opposite of suicide is to undertake the impossible, to live the contradiction of a memory that is immemorable, of a demand for adequacy that cannot adequately be met, and of an assistance of the other when one's own needs are running sores. The meaning and owning of ethics signify the act of being empty-handed, feeling accused, obedient (but to no one else), and to suffer the consequences.

To initial the disruption in the script of one's effort is to be an initiate of the ethical. It is to owe nothing to any officiate since there is no other than oneself, the subject, subject to one's own obedience. It is also not to be overly passive in expectation of the unexpected stop of consciousness, but to seek ways and means of instituting the stop on one's own. Since disruption defies ends, means, and reason, initiation is endless improvisation, the opposite of continuous perfection of technique. How to initiate disruption of self-constituting consciousness and the perpetual recreation of essential signification, like how to make rest move, cannot be solved intellectually but only by somatic contact and proximity. To put on the mantle of originlessness, to be orphaned of being, outcast, accused, is to be wary of the wiles of initiation. Although one makes efforts at cultivation, no one initiates one, not even oneself, since one is chosen, elected, and ordained by that which is far beyond one's own power. Receptivity, not reflexivity, is a determinant, and because of that, efforts to begin where there is no beginning are useful insofar as they sympathetically draw forth a true force of disruption—one string made to vibrate at the same pitch as another already vibrating in proximity. Because the trial of the ethical is continual, its outcome remains a question. In the total trajectory of its quest lies a useful measure of the success of subjectivity.

At its origin, essence too is initiated and brought to a promise of its own disclosure, thereby inducting signification and the ring of signs into the ceremony of meaning. As essence stands forth, known in its nakedness by a nakedness of knowing—percipience—it is greeted as co-respondent to subjectivity, and the subject to essence. In the encounter, the arche name is voiced in utterance of the primal sentence, "*That I am.*" Although co-respondents together, the two particles, essence and subject, arche name and being, do not stand as equals on the same footing, but as unequals on different footings. My embrace of suchness evokes a turning of *that* toward *I*, but not necessarily a reciprocal embrace since correspondence is not identical with mutuality. Welcoming, dwelling, presence, and openness itself are clauses of the initiatic vow, made actual (along with their contraries) for consciousness and being in the world by the selfsame point of origination. Let be at home, the subject is granted poise and dignity by belonging to an order, a household, an arrangement of beings, as one who is steward. Neither lord nor owner, subjectivity is charged to keep the signs and significations—the unveilings—safe from harm, although at the same time the mystery of the veil is withheld. The only dispensation is that the mystery of the mystery can be rendered more essentially, with a greater reverence that is in keeping with our role. Of a saying that concerns all that can be said, Heidegger says, "We must think *aletheia*, unconcealment, as the opening which first brings Being and thinking and their presencing to and for each other."[1] Only essence, the initiate, is brought into the mystery of manifestation, and for this reason, human knowledge shares in the light and joy of sympathy without shouldering any of the responsibility of disclosure. It is radiant in the light of unveiling without knowing the words that miraculously draw the veil apart.

The ontological work of subjectivity devolves from a vow not the subject's own: the sympathetic expression of essence. To gather and keep the revelations of being, consciousness grips designation so tightly that it becomes a substitute for the sign. In the process of becoming a sign, a sign of transparency among other transparent signs, self-knowledge is strictly delimited by subjectivity's relation to essence—assistant or steward. That the subject is not a candidate for initiation, that it is not a responsible one, that its consciousness must remain exoteric, means that knowledge of subjectivity is knowledge of a missing person, an alias, a disguise, a someone not real. The power of a "pure original unchangeable consciousness" of Kant's transcendental apperception and his treatment of the paralogisms of pure reason, derive from acknowledgment of this limiting factor.[2] Likewise, the redefinition of the subject as spontaneity (following from the Third Antinomy) is a rearguard defense of anemia, inertia, and noninitiation. Both approaches incline toward pessimism and despair (or worse, Hume's solution) when they demonstrate the poverty of substituting an analytic identity for the flesh and blood of subjectivity. If there were only the work of ontology, the safeguarding of meaning in a home not one's own, then contentment or infinite resignation could buoy the subject up in the face of an ignorance as to "why," so that like Mill's good utilitarian, the happiness of a pig counts more than the knowledge of Socrates.

Since to seek initiation in the beyond-being is to quest after that which precedes manifestation and the dialectic of love, there is a work superior to ontology. The door to mystery opens with the inauspicious and unpropitious, when the loveliness of meaning is suddenly dispelled and its charm broken. The other, in this disruption, stands in front of me, a beggar, whether in rags or riches. To welcome the unwelcome, to bring him or her in, to tend to the suffering, to lift up the downcast brow—the elements of an initiate act have no signification if it is not to turn the unexpected away with explanation, erudition, and autonomy. Since that which takes precedence wears the poorest and thinnest of coats, its proximity is disregarded, its running sores dismissed. Because the disruption that subordinates essence and meaning is always uninvited, to meet it cannot involve the appropriative gesture, it cannot be made one's own. To face the leper, the pariah, the Sudra, with welcome, to relinguish one's place at the table and place the other in one's place, are acts that pave the way toward initiation. They are acts of intense, selfless listening, a listening for the categorical voice in the melee of reaction, disappointment, repulsion, egoism. Abiding in the way of disruption, collecting no signs (since none are offered), one finds that the door to what takes precedence opens a crack, and what is higher enters.

Commotion outside the gate and an uninvited guest—Alcibiades—is ushered in and made welcome. Though his brusqueness disrupts the discourse, he does not bring the ethical in his own person but calls it forth in the other: "The same old game of lying in wait and popping out at me when I least expect you."[3] It is Socratic genius to stand between dismissal and welcome, in the gap disruption opens, searching out an initiating force different from meaning and the ego. If found, such a force neither dismisses dismissal nor welcomes welcome, but remembers from "within things themselves" that the matter of the matter is the imperative voice that categorically resounds in every thought, word, or deed. Such a force—the ethical itself—answers the other's disruption in the only tongue equal to the task: it disrupts the disruption with a touch at the elbow, leading the other to one's own place, standing behind to assist the other. The ethical initiates a response to disruption by extinguishing the self-constituting autonomous ego, and attending to the exigence exposed. It exposes subjectivity and thereby grants the subject the responsibility of transforming (not palliating) the other's suffering to a longing for what is higher. Thus exposed and in contact with the other's pain, the subject meets an obligation older than decision and more binding than choice. The ethical obligation to suffer the crude, coarse, vulgar, and profane in the other's suffering and to lift it up and refine it is, therefore, a double obligation. One must bring a twofold help to the other, outer and inner, even when the two actions move in different directions. One cannot be stinting in help, one must give the other one's own place and at the same time witness that the other does not suffer in vain. One is summoned to the transformatory power of sacrifice.

That in the bloated belly, broken back, and tortured figure of the victim is the initiatic matter of ethics in a demonstration of its indemonstrability. Riveted by the call, accused, judged and found wanting, I am wakened from a living death to a life in which the other's life hangs on my every breath. He/she is not the same as I, and as I bear witness to the difference, giving the other my place, I recognize his/her torment as a troubled gift, a disguised blessing, by which the other also may stand before the disruptive call of ethics. Not now, since the other is a captive of pain, but sometime. Then, the doubling of help will be apparent, wherein I tend the other's running sores at the same time I give testimony to their purpose vis-à-vis the other's purpose. The touch at the elbow, opening the door to my house, rescuing another from hooded assailants, also speak of the secret signification of the initiate, for to be an initiate is to seek to initiate others. By my touch do I bring the other, though in pain, in closer proximity to the call of ethics. By my showing the other in do I bring the other, though suffering greatly, closer to an obedience whose recognition surpasses the ontological, whose recognition is of the timeless and ahistorical.

13

SUFFERING AND THE PASSIVITY OF THE SUBJECT

Disruption, a nonevent that breaks the stream of occurrence, is suffered by the subject. But disruption does not inhere in a patient, the one who suffers, like a property or mode; nor is it a disease unless pregnancy is counted as one. Breaking up the gesture of appropriation that makes meaning one's own, disruption opens the abyss of meaninglessness where, stripped of protection, exposed, one can do no other than heed the fact of obligation. Since the act of attention eo ipso implies subservience, one places oneself under an obligation that waits more patiently than a patient, accepts subordination, ceases to ferret out signification, and does as commanded by the commandment. Disintegrating the protective shield of meaning, disruption addresses the subject as alteration, the way of the other, a deviation from the chosen course of action, a divination of novelty. Abraham has all the confidence of self-making in his freedom as he stretches forth his hand and takes the knife to slay his son. In the thicket of accomplishment, in the transparency of purpose, when the "I think" can accompany thought and action, Abraham finds himself in the company of the unexpected, undesired, inconceivable otherness. "And the angel of the Lord called unto him out of heaven and said, 'Abraham, Abraham': and he said, 'Here am I.'" Since the only answer to the imperative voice that categorically erupts in the midst of a predicament is the arche name, disruption is suffered in order to give birth to the *who* who is capable of uttering the "*I am.*"

Since disruptive force is against time and space, without point of origin, lacking all coordinates, it moves neither from here to there, nor to and from, nor back and forth. The subject that suffers disruption suffers a directionless force that steals directedness from thought and leaves consciousness trembling and disoriented. A knock at the door, a phone call, the flight of birds, an ache in the chest, a yen for a drink, a shiver, a petty memory, a thought of tomorrow, a broken melody, wind in one's ear, ennui, fatigue, a recurrent dream, an itch, the thumping of one's own finger—disruption meets the occasion in different guises but always with the sowing of difference. In the suspended interval when one is a patient, in the desert when one is without direction and signpost, the opportunity for allying or alligning oneself with the disruptive spirit calls. Not distracted, derailed, or disspirited by the break in the course of things, one recollects from "within things themselves" that one is an unprofitable servant, subject to duty, irregular in its discharge, indigent, unserviceable—and in remorse, renews one's vow to seek initiation where none are masters and all are ignorant. When the will, whose hyperextention is for Descartes the cause of error, bows down, consciousness is in readiness, and the listening in the somatic depths ready to hear the imperative, "Abraham, Abraham." Because in the state of atonement or atunement, the problem of meaning has been extinguished, from extinction arises the voice of the arche name, *"I am."* Attaching signification to no thing, *"I am"* is the bald utterance of availability. "I am now prepared to serve." Subordinate, helper, assistant to a creation ever in need of renewal, subjectivity feels its indebted condition in the deafening thunder of the unconditional, and takes up the yoke of ethics.

Suffering is the interval of incomprehension occasioned by disruption as well as, beyond that, the responsibility of comprehension. When the stream of occurrence is ruptured and whether the signlessness of the desert produces anxiety, vertigo, or rapture, subjectivity is met with passivity, the reopening of its woundedness, exposure, aridness. Not able, the subject suffers its own lack of initiative, of responsiveness, in the face of the nonevent that has superceded all events, that is, in the face of the other. Since disruption cannot occur in solitude, since it is the other that interrupts the one, subjectivity suffers in the other's presence its inability to trade places with the other, to give the other its last penny, to bind the other's wound with the shirt off one's back. When this paralysis, this "being stung by the goad," evokes acceptance of its opacity, when denial of suffering ceases, absence of initiative eo ipso engenders an effort. That passivity in the face of suffering is able to respond to otherness with an alteration of suffering is precisely the mystery over which ethics officiates. That suffering is transformed (but not palliated) by my recognition of unresponsiveness to give birth to responsibility is the mystery into which I wish to be initiated. Since, aware or not, subjectivity suffers indebtedness, the comprehension of responsibility does not eliminate cost but pares the repayment of encumbrances. That one suffers mechanically from the restlessness of desire and a general lack of attainment means that dissatisfaction colors consciousness, signification, and the progressive loss and recovery of self. That essentialism and the work of ontology is impregnated with such suffering is the meaning of Spinoza's proposition that desire is the essence of humanity.[1] Since the dark spell of refusal and resistance is broken by the face of the other, beseeching and undignified, subjectivity submits to a transformation, a recollection, and a subordination. It grows heavy with initiative and takes the reins over self-will. No longer blinded in its God-driven act, it is stopped by the voice of what takes precedence, and turning to the fright on the other's, its own son's face, utters the arche name. No longer obsessed by a pact with itself to hide its fear of disruption, it turns heavenward to receive a gift from what is higher. Far from decreasing with the transformation of refusal to responsibility, the weight on subjectivity actually increases in step with the increased potency. While responsibility is more grave, has more gravity, than does refusal, it potentizes the subject like no other can. Responsibility, taking the other in and giving the other my place, adds the other's weight to mine, exercising and extending my power to bear what needs to be borne in subjectivity. Responsibility potentizes like signification cannot since it is authorless, without authority, anarchic while meaning is authored by essence and, therefore, limited and finite. Since the responsible one is bound by no meaning or ontological work and is responsible to no master or to a masterless master, that one is unbounded and infinite.

Since to undergo privation of initiative is the way of initiation into the ethical, the ethical is a logos of suffering, a patho-logy. The inner dynamics of the patient, the one whose composure is threatened with dissolution, progressively deepen the contact with the other, in face of whom suffering takes place. As the responsibility of taking in the other, offering him/her one's own place, is more fully met, blame is exonerated without lessening one's liability. Although the trope of disease seems to incline ethics toward a "sickness unto death," a progressive debilitation of a will to life, privation has in fact the opposite effect. Contact with what is absent, the not-there, the *Nichtdasein*, is the enigma, the unlocking of which opens the way to initiation. Dis-ease, the negative of the ease of being, is disquiet, exposure, vulnerability, subjugation—the opposite of a positive positing or positioning. Above all, it is a willingness to be directed instead of a directing, a giving over to the direction of the other, his/her weakness, deprivation, or fear. In contact with a lack of initiative, I find insubordination and inferiority to what takes precedence, and from my inattentiveness arises a force able to disrupt my impotence with the potency of what is higher.

Since inattentiveness and unconscientiousness belong to the opaque, to speak them illuminates no thing—in contrast to the way the ghostly light of transcendental apperception does the object. The logos of privation and suffering is that of night, when thought gives over to prayer. A knowledge of the self in this milieu similarly lacks substance, transparency, signifyingness, and (one could almost say), the subject—Eckhart's "efface yourself as completely as if you did not exist."[2] A privative knowledge or a positive ignorance of the mysterious influx speaks of the trace of the higher in its exchange with the inferior in conundrum and riddle but not in theme or representation. That which is without origin has never yet presented itself to consciousness and, therefore, cannot be represented. That from which initiative is drawn is the anomolous, the deviation from rule, method, and analogy that defies logic, in the way that the imperative to give the other my place defies the logic of self-interest and utility. It is also drawn from the anonymous, lacking name as well as identity, since the first name, the arche name *I*, comes already in response to a nameless, nounless, substantiveless imperative. The superior remains as an unthematizable trace, an uplifting of the heart in the vale of tears, that without aspiring to presence is never a nullity. Inasmuch as its nonpresence—its passing over, as the angel of death did those doorposts marked with a sign—can be said to cause initiation, the superior is beyond presence and this very absence of presence draws forth (as a vacuum does to objects) an initiating response. Even the term *absence of presence* marks the assymptote toward which the line of superiority approaches without meeting as well as its incommensurability with the subject. Because it passes over, is immeasurable, and partakes of nothing, the superior is an omnipresent influence, the "one behind the scenes," with a hand in everything. Inasmuch as, like an induction coil, it is action at an immeasurable distance, the superior induces and initiates without presence just as it commands without a book of the law.

The patience of subjectivity is more passive than passivity because it does not flinch at the absence of reason, cause, and predication that it suffers. Its suffering is not a pure undergoing—the way innocence suffers at the hand of evil—but an impure one—the way the justly accused suffers. Since its suffering is a making up for a deficit, it is remorse and atonement, not the glad suffering for a death from an incurable and pain-wracking illness. Furthermore, it is suffering not contingent on a state of being, as though attainment to essence were equal to release or deliverance. That proper comportment in being wins a freedom from the pain of pain is a transcendental illusion of essentialism. Suffering is the systole of life just as enjoying is the diastole. The pain of pain is irretractible because subjectivity is commanded by a voice that is unprincipled and without rules. The content of ethics, therefore, is not a set of principles that orders "the moral life" like a syllogism, producing transparency and moral discourse. Nor is it a mode of judgment (*a la* Solomon) that weighs desire and duty in quasidivine scales in order to arrive at enlightened action. Ethics has no content other than a momentary summons in which an immemorable memory pricks the compassionate heart to recall the other's exigence. The more nearly empty, the more proximate and vulnerable the subject is. Unlike ontology whose subject is a *that*, the subject of ethics is the subject. The subject is a *who* almost perforated to a zero by a categorical summons. *Who* that subject is more nearly vanishes the closer to responsibility it approaches. Perfect emptiness has no more a text than has a response perfectly informed by the raw surface exposed to the other's inner need.

The pain I speak of is distinct from a *Weltschmertz*, an affliction of creatures as existing. Although much has been made of angst, nausea, and vertigo—the noncoincidence of essence (which is to say, desire) and existence—nonetheless the pain of alteration is different. The pain of alteration is the pain of alternation. The abrupt shift from freedom and self-legislation to subordination and lawlessness (and back again) is doubly painful in that it throws autonomy into question at the same time that it elevates the exception above the rule. When the supremacy of autonomy is challenged and competition with heteronomy renewed, the separateness by which ego identifies ego becomes sharper and more real. Along with an insurgent heteronomy come the chains of conditions and contingencies that isolate the self-caused consciousness from the other. Because consciousness is obsessed with the unconditioned, its fear of the uncaused nonevent, it is preoccupied by the dialectic operation that Kant calls the "antinomy of pure reason": "if the conditioned is given, the entire series of all its conditions is likewise given.[3] The nervous glance toward a totality that is nonexistent, the reverse side of objects, the dark face of the moon, states the neurosis of heteronomy. Although autonomy is more desirable because, being a law unto itself, its desires are more attainable, nonetheless its greater transparency suffers greater ruin from the categorical voice. The lawlessness of the imperative, the unpredictable accusation of the other, the other's unsatisfiable exigence, all break the circle of autonomy without appeal to adjudication. That anarchy is without judges and the anarchaic force that takes precedence conveys a freedom in obedience makes the return to autonomy different from an unbroken autonomy. In that difference lies the specific suffering that is ethical.

To carry the memory that cannnot be remembered is the task of the ethical subject. Since to stay in promixity with that which cannot be represented or signified demands ardor, resourcefulness, and courage—a "barehanded" approach—subjectivity is vulnerable to the reproaches of forgetting. Who is not a Hamlet scored for his "almost blunted purpose" and who is able to be reminded by the beggar who upbraids the world for its evils? The dis-ease of the ethical, its interruptedness, can be brought to no curative pitch unless one suffers one's unprofitability and cultivates a suffering for the forgotten task. Since not to forget is to be reminded by the disruptive other, in whatever guise it takes, the work requires deepening contact and sensitivity—a somatic work. That the ethical requires a cultivation of the soma and the subtle body is evident in Aristotle's thought that a practical syllogism ends in an action. Exposure of the interior of subjectivity and its woundedness has a "mnemonic" value inasmuch as my own running sore reminds me of the other's and his/her exigence.

Although saintliness alone may be able to welcome the categorical accusation, the ethical subject moved by it to ease its resistance is a responsible one. The commandment does not command the "pure heart," only the one accused by the other's lame walk, jaundiced pallor, or malnourished look.

Although the weightless weight of memory is ungraspable, the heart of sympathy can be sympathetically struck by the memory's absence, and resound. The distinction between election or dint of effort evaporates in the heat of remembrance because one remembers that one has not remembered. The accusative of forgetfulness is the objective case of the other who never forgets to remember, who lives in the pain of memory and suffers the indignity of being forgotten. "I have forgotten" and "I have been forgotten," active and passive, blame and incrimination, find a unity where myself and the other are interchangeable. A lapse in memory and I am without contact with what takes precedence, isolated and solitudinous. No longer remembered, I am both victim and perpetrator, analogous to how, when I obey, I am both commander and commanded. Forgotten and forgetful, I have inadvertently placed myself in the shoes of the other—I am other than myself—and now await my redemption in the sympathetic hands of the other. An alien in my own skin, a stranger crawling out of my skin, I am a nobody until taken in by disruptive memory, and shown the other's place, offered as my own.

14

EFFORT AND PRAXIS

The memory that remembers itself is always late. Phenomenologically, memory comes upon itself under cover of lethe, already *in medias res* having gathered remembrance to a certain degree. At the point at which oblivion congeals, disruption is already underway and the matter of its origin, nonexistent, ephemeral. The congelation of oblivion is also the point at which one recognizes that suffering is being and has been undergone. That the being of suffering is a precursor of memory (Nietzsche's discovery) and that suffering intensifies memory and makes it incandescent means that remembrance is necessarily patience, a passivity that actively seizes opportunities of disruption. Patience is also vulnerability to weakness since it is given to lapses and digressions without ceasing to be constant in attendance. In the constancy of its exposure, patience proves that it can remember itself without becoming apparent—though we must not call it a dispositional term, thinking that we have added something to its identity. The intangibility of this patient memory, this memory of patience, suffers the shock of its condition at the hands of an outside force, a prod exterior to the consistent vigil. Because disruption surpasses memory, breaking remembrance and disrememberance alike, it is the immemorable and impatience. In surfacing from the stream of lethe, memory meets not only itself but an impatience of the other-than-itself. Memory suffers an impatience not its own, is accused and found wanting by impatience, and is required patiently to suffer this alien impatience.

The bearing of memory is praxis. The order to carry a memory that cannot be borne, cannot be punctual, and encounters an alien recrimination is not commanded by a prior commitment, earlier decision, or chosen way of being. Nor is it the result of the Stoic command to be free from passion, nor the Gnostic command to suffer the indignities of a human life for a final liberation, nor the command of a good will that is "good without qualification."[1] Although the command comes from outside, from across the field, it is uttered by the lips of the one commanded and sealed with the insignia of that one's heart. Although from outside, the command to remember is to remember to take the stranger *in*, to trade places with the other from another land. Since to advance the lot of the other, to bind the wounds and fill the belly, is only half of the double obligation, one must also remember the commandment to bring remembrance to the other. It is insufficient to remember the other's utility since the higher part of remembering the other concerns that which runs counter to self-interest, both for the one and the other. The Kantian mark of categoricality, the "renunciation of all interest," is appropriate since law making altogether must come to a stop.[2] Although to feed, clothe, and shelter the pauper is a good turn and commendable as such, unless the other's memory of surpassingness is stirred, I have not brought myself fully into remembrance, have not exposed myself to the other as the other has to me, and so, remain condescendingly and patronizingly aloof.

The ambitiousness of memory is perfection: to say that it has remembered. The ambiguity of memory is that remembrance takes place in the praxis of passivity, without the subject's undertaking anything at all. The autoproduction of consciousness, its obsession with a signification that dispels its fear of discontinuity, its self-lapsing and self-recovery, supplies no impetus for remembering, unless concealment itself is. The imperative voice that summons remembering and adds the reverberation of the arche name "*I am*" to the event breaks up the clouds of self-interest like a whirlwind. Though outside, the categorical mood is felt as one's own, but with a signification that differs from that of a co-responding sign. The categoricality of command lies in its being one's own as other than one's own. Its ambiguity also consists in being the-other-in-the-one, its surpassing the one with the prick of a memory of difference. Because it does not signify like essence, its meaning is not referrable to the totality of signs ringed round. This nonreferrable meaning has "no place to go" inasmuch as it is not a cipher or substitute for another, as in the case of heteronomous meaning. Not referrable, incapable of being made one's own, inappropriatable, the meaning commanded of memory is eo ipso is driven in every direction or none. This root ambiguity or undecipherability is both volatability and potency.

Ethical praxis is thus highly ambitious and ambiguous. Inasmuch as both qualities leave it open to charges of sophistry (incomplete memory) and fascism (presumptive memory), a little praxis is a dangerous thing. To the exposure wrought by the disruptive commandment, the reaction of ego, in which consciousness is suited up in more impenetrable armor than ever, is likely. The self-calming play of consciousness feigns disruption, moving from loss to recovery, in order to disarm the commandment in advance. In order for the play to catch "the conscience of a king," the effort at patience cannot be contrived, precious, or forced without jeopardizing the outcome. The overcoming of self-possession requires the subtlety of a body that is subtle since the mysterious transaction through which memory becomes incarnate takes place in the life body. Release *from* self—self-legislating, self-narrating, and self-calming—is release *to* the somatic logos which alone in subjectivity is capable of contact with an alogical disruption. That soma is able to undergo and be patient in the face of impatience is because of its temporal sensitivity. It knows time, not as an a priori form of intuition, a precondition for running off phenomena, but as timing. Somatic timing—rhythm, tempo, pulse, accent, meter, recurrences that signify movement in time—is a respiration, a systole and diastole, that is complete in "knowing" that the sequel to a depletion is a repletion. Since the fullness of forgetting follows and is followed by the emptiness of memory, soma is able to abide in patience, in passivity, in an effort that is noneffort, for the recurrence of remembering.

The dissolution of self-interest—dis-interest—is not equivalent to its annihilation since interest itself is transformed and refined in the breath of the higher. The principle of self-interest, whether hedonic or enlightened, is shattered in the midst of its calculus by an unprincipled voice that in demanding a suspension of self demands a return to the root meaning of interest, the *inter-esse*, the exchange. Disinterest differs sharply from fellow-feeling, the creatureliness of community, in that one is not asked to calculate the other's interest from the other's viewpoint or from the viewpoint of an abstract, general happiness, but to come to the viewpoint of what takes precedence. Disinterest is not an attainment or operation of calculation at all because it is the disruption of the calculative mind, the break in the stream of occurrence, the schism between two events, Eckhart's "empty nothingness."[3] Totality of exposure and of vulnerability dissolves resistance and refusal to admitting the other to my place, opening the door to my house to the other, bathing his/her wounds with my tears. The stirring of disinterest from the compassionate heart "can do no other"—the signification of obedience to the categorical voice. It is a signification that makes reference to no other sign and that exists apart from the totality of signs. Since, like sympathy, disinterest evokes likeness in response, my own subordination to what takes precedence is felt by the other as a lifting up, an elevation, or an exaltation. Thus does memory breed memory, memory of the other in the one breeding memory of the one in the other.

Disinterest arises from trauma like a phoenix from ashes. An injury to self-will that temporarily releases one from commitment and conditions opens the way to a suspension of self-interest. The "I think" that shadows every event, monitoring it for conformity to self, is shucked, and the tender underskin of the soma sensitized to the exigence of the situation. Memory remembers how to dispel separateness and to become appreciative of the potentization of subjectivity. The potentized subject is able to bear greater depths of exposure as well as to express greater interest in what is higher. Potency does not arrive progressively, in a smooth curve, but abruptly, in a quantum leap. The diverse magnitudes in a "leap of faith" do not compromise the all-at-once force of potency, but speak to different advents. Potentized, subjectivity responds disinterestedly, without calculus, induction, or extrapolation, the way the left hand responds to pull the right hand away from the fire. In that sense, there can be no praxis of disinterest any more than of disruption—or if there is, it concerns availability and recollection. The unpracticability of any praxis proposed and the absence of any method intended, make speaking about the attainment of disinterest meaningless. Depending on the potency of subjectivity, I respond to the other's open sores with care and solace, or with disregard.

Succussion, a violent shake up, potentizes the subject, making it fit for ethical undertaking. The radical disjunction of otherness, its recurrent proof of the Nichtsdasein, repeatedly exposes the soma to an energizing far beyond that of its life. Having no beginning or bounds, this energy surpasses any of essence and leaves its sympathetic influence on the somatic tissue, just as the angel of death affects even the houses of those it passes over. Since alertness and awakenness follow in its wake, the subject is able to live in a memory alien to subjectivity, an alien memory, a memory other than reminiscence. Overturning the law-abiding state of consciousness and leaving a state of war, the wake of disruption thus reveals a latency of the subject that can be disclosed in no other way. This disclosure constitutes the primordial meaning of the ethical and communicates itself sympathetically to all positions and propositions that belong to the ethical, the way a symphonic theme speaks to every movement of the piece, guiding melody and rhythm by its absence as well as its presence. The latency concerns the possibility of providing a home for the impermanent, destabilizing, anarchical energy that potentizes the subject—to become as it were a waystation for the homeless. It also concerns borrowing a power that (unlike that of life) is never loaned, that belongs to a life within one's life more naked than nakedness. Since to increase the borrowing power, borrowing the unlendable, actualizes the life of the other within oneself, one's mortality is altered. The life of the other does not return to origin since it does not arise originarily. Being other, it is its own life and is not on loan. The potentized subject in the moment of disruption knows the taste of immortality and knows that taste can be deepened to infinity with infinitely deepened exposure.

If it can be spoken of at all, the way to immortality leads through a renunciation of changelessness and a sacrifice of the permanence of signification. The fixed stars of the empyrean—the designata—are called to return to cosmic dust and the whirlwind of strife that mixes all meanings. When the unchanging ego that navigates by the familiar constellations suffers exposure to the ambiguous and opaque, it gives way to a patience of passivity that is continual receptivity and adaptation to disruption—and is effaced. The noncoincidence between the patient one and the battering suffered at the hands of disruption is what potentizes subjectivity and relegates ego to a specialized position. To be found by the imperative voice and to let the categorical render one disinterested, subjectivity must already have exercised anarchaic power over ego and the sway of signification. Immortality is the recurrence of exercise. Inasmuch as the face of the other that bades me trade places is the occasion of exercise, immortality cannot be spoken of my own and is not personal. If Kant understands the unspeakability of immortality as having to do with its otherness, then the immortal is unspeakable because it belongs to no person. It is impersonal without being nominative like the herd, the mass, *das Man*, or the one. If an aspect of subjectivity survives death, that aspect has nothing to do with *my* life, but a life alien to mine, a life outside mine that I take in by giving up my place, my comfort, and surety, and risking everything to be responsible in the other's place. Since the survival of that aspect stems from the fact that it has never come to existence, afterdeath survival has nothing to do with me—or any other person. Only the Other in whose care and sympathy the life other than life is entrusted knows the intermittency of immortality. The episodic character of creation, moved by the mystery of exchange, constitutes the esoteric knowledge into which an initiate is inducted, upon attaining the requisite degree of potentization.

By hyperbole or obfuscation, one can say that praxis involves no-effort. Although the ethical is a disruption to the busyness of the for-itself, the autoproduction of consciousness, and the repeated instantiation of the "I think," the gap does not "just happen." That alteration involves a search implies volition and care on the part of the seeker. The quest for the other, the meeting of which is exchange, moves from strength to strength, the root meaning of *effort*. By force of effort, disruption can be called, culled, and cultivated. Just as the culture of otherness differs from the cult of the same precisely by the increment of effort, so does devotion differ from idolatry. To fawn over the other's immiseration or curry the other's pain without tending to his/her exigence makes an idol of poverty and thereby marginalizes or trivializes a real moral dilemma. To weep crocodile tears or cough up blood money is to deny the accusation voiced by the other's indigence, broken heart, or bleeding wound. It is to evade part of the responsibility of lifting up the other from the gutter and giving over one's own coat for warmth, that is, to evade the responsibility, period.

Since it is not a contraction, a flexing, a relapse into closure and instrumentality, effort has the force of trial beyond trying. Trying, the intentionality of consciousness, has nothing to do with an obedience that is (in Marcel's words) the *epreuve*. An ethical proof is not syllogistic, inductive, or modal because it comes as a reproof to a calculative predisposition. Nor is proof in the ethical a matter of commitment or the decisive moment, since the other's presence has the force of a counterproof or exception to proof. The test tests a capability to abide in the face of the unabiding difference of otherness, not to collapse the other into equality and sameness. The abidingness, a strength of the undying life within subjective life, meets the other and soothes the other's wounds and salves the other's soul with undying compassion. The other, healed and made whole, then can dwell in the thought of what takes precedence—just as I was motivated by it. Or, the other, incurable and remaining fragmented, curses the higher, damns it with his/her damnation, and leaves me thwarted in my effort. In either case, I have been tried and, within limits, found unexpiated, indebted, irresponsible—lacking proof that an undying memory is incarnate in my soma, that I have been initiated into the mystery of exchange, that I entertain a serious question about the *who* of the other. Precisely within my rebuke lies hope of proof if the tremor of acceptance meets the firm imperative voice.

15

CONSCIENCE

The destabilization of ego's authoritarianism proceeds by trial of subjectivity. Since the trying of the trial, which can recur at any moment, from any direction, without apparent cause, is not reducible to reason, the charges remain unarticulated. They are there to meet the subject when it wakes from dreams, feels its own skin, or is angered by its own insolence—as if they could outwait consciousness and stood ready for the first move. The enigma of the ethical trial lies in the discrepancy or noncoincidence of responsibility and capability, of indebtedness and net worth. Dostoevsky's observation from the mouth of the Grand Inquisitor resounds: "Instead of giving a firm foundation for setting the conscience of man at rest forever, Thou didst choose all that is exceptional, vague, and enigmatic." That disruption finds the subject closed in on itself, defensive, self-interested, and isolated is a signification of the trial and its enigma. Since the subject's life can be hedonically or eudaemonically correct and still subject to trial, no system of social justice or method of judicial meaning quells the fire of disruption. One's protestation of innocence in the face of a charge of injustice is also an expression of the ethical enigma because refusal replaces welcome in the advent of that which is higher. One willingly substitutes the lower for the higher, in the Grand Inquisitor's words, "Choosing 'bread,' Thou wouldst have satisfied the universal and everlasting craving of humanity . . ."

If the trial of subjectivity merely produced protestation or the passivity of resignation, the ethical would hold it hostage solely for humilation and debasement. Then ethics would be the faceless captor of a humanity that falls into its trap at birth, a pessimism that has no bottom, that says, "A short life is better, best is not to be born at all." Then a rejection of the ethical force of disruption would constitute the just response of a pragmatic understanding of signification. Since disruption puts meaning on trial, interposing an enigma between the sign and the signified, the signification of being the accused, being addressed in the accusative, comes into question. The hesitancy between designation and substitution by synonomy—the hyphen of the out breath—is patience, the allowance of the imperative to command. In the resounding sound of categoricality, subjectivity again faces the ethical face and finds it in proximity. In that sound, distance is avoidance, and avoidance—not of the abstract but of my neighbor's face—that guise that disruption puts on when it tries me. The sphinx face of enigma that rewrites signification cuts ego short in the midst of self-absorption, rubs gratingly against its presumption, and commands absolute obedience to a meaning as yet not unfolded.

Unless the "exceptional, vague, and enigmatic" is heard and obeyed, the ethical is a muted pang of sympathy, indistinguishable from an itch, prick, or flush. Blind obedience is a contradiction in terms since the trial consists in conformation to a disruptive force known to be an intercession to reason, thought, and consciousness. If a subject obeys blindly, a good deed may result, but not a pure heart. The command of the ethical is to stand trial, not to be exonerated, rescinded, released, or paroled. Since what subjectivity has not committed or willed cannot be pardoned, the ethical is the unpardonable. The patience of passivity required to meet the abrasively vague and indeterminately signifying is what leads the way to potentization. The subject susceptible to potentization is the one who bears the trial with the recognition that effort leads to effort, strength to strength, and that the point is not to terminate the examination but extend it to infinity. One subject to the ethical is one who, in response and responsibility, bears witness to the infinite other in humanity.

The enigma that is the infinitesimal delay between sign and signified, designation and referent is enigmatic because it does not present itself, can never present itself since it belongs to a past that was never present. Memory of the immemorable past is kindled by a spark of the enigmatic that resides in subjectivity like secret aspiration. Since the imperceptible hesitation within custom and automation is itself an entire approach to signification, it cannot be accepted in degree, tentatively, on a trial basis, or in installments. Categories of quantity and quality apply to names and essence, are the instruments of metaphysics, but have no play in the ethical. Either one listens to the riddling heartbeat between signification and comprehension, or not. To be riddled about one's identity and to bear the charge of alias and crime is to have the "I think" placed in question. The *who* that trades places with the other is ready to heed the voice that tries all indicatives and accuses all nominatives, that in its categoricality commands the singular response, "*I am.*" Only the *who* that utters the arche name in the throes of disruption is responsible.

The enigma is that the ethical has been but is not now or ever. It also is that the ethical lies in passing or surpassing of the present yet is always already past. Of a past beyond remoteness, that never was present, the enigma is to consciousness as what lies undisinterrable is to the light. It is, therefore, appropriate that the trope of an "organ" buried within the ground of consciousness or of an Atlantean culture swallowed by the earth represents the enigma that is conscience. It is also appropriate that in some languages conscience is not distinguished from consciousness since conscience is not a faculty, capability, function, aptitude, or portion of consciousness. Kant's attempt to place conscience on a rational footing not only ignores the phenomenology of conscience but elevates autonomy to the level of a demigod. To say "conscience is practical reason holding man's duty before him wherever a law is applicable" is to draw the infinite in the scale of the finite, to divide one by zero and call the solution "rational."[1] Motivation for the reconturing comes from the assignment of existence and facticity to conscience. Kant speaks of conscience as an actual fact present to a subject, whereas absence of conscience is precisely what allows the mysterious transformation that ignites the fire of conscience in the subject. The privation of conscience evokes responsibility, awareness of the fact of obligation—that obligation is the matrix of subjectivity and not the converse. With the first neonatal breath, the subject breathes in the obligation that awaits it with a patience greater than passivity. With that inspiration is born an aspiration to the path of conscience.

The work of conscience belongs to the interval in which the enigma recurs. Never done and when undertaken, undertaken late, the work of meeting otherness, its exceptional and surpassing singularity, consists in no planned response—when no response may be unconscionable. Conscience, a fully potentized subjectivity, and a realization that to trade places with the other is to place the other under the same obligation the subject is subject to, go hand in hand. The enigma of the noncongruence of signification and essence is worked out in the contact of exchange. The meaning of the ethical is achieved by igniting the ashes of the other's flame by the heat of one's own initiative. Although recurrent loss of meaning speaks to the pastness of conscience, the other, helped by the shirt off my back, is helped surpassingly by the memory my dignity ignites in him. Ethical signification never offers "bread" without the challenge of measuring the exception by that which in a subject is exceptional.

The vagueness intrinsic to ethical signification in relation to signification by essence lends it both its aporetic and oracular qualities. From singularity to singularity, it cannot be torn from the saying in which it is said without distorting the said. In its root meaning, ethical signification is utterance—audible expression—that is related, through the Greek radical *ai-* to *enigma*. Severely contextual, spoken for one "who hath ears to hear," imperative in mood, ethical meaning disrupts the hermeneutics of essence with a hermeneutics more ancient than that of origin. Since the utterance both summons and names, the subject is called by its proper name in the accusative ("Abraham, Abraham") and responds with the affirmation of responsibility contained in the arche name, *I*. In the cycle of call and response, the act of creation is recreated. The imperative voice of the categorical resounds from a past that was never a present and is met by a speaker who announces present existence. Anarchy meets origin, beginningless time meets the initial explosion of time, unmanifest meets manifest, infinity meets zero. Since the delay between address and reply corresponds to the hesitancy between sign and signified, the interval of enigma, during which the mystery of exchange is reenacted, is an irreplaceable feature of ethical signification. Although the call proceeds by proper name ("Abraham"), and although the vocalization is not the same as that in discourse and dialectic, the call does not, as Heidegger says, call "solely and constantly in the mode of keeping silent."[2] Silence is not so much the imperatival other to the indicative mood as the elimination of all indications save one, the silent. To empty discourse of all matters of demonstration, ostentation, and suggestion and to let the remainder "speak" is to give a mutism ethical authority. Not in discourse, nor even in silent discourse, is the proper name called with a force sufficient to empty the ego of imperialism, but only through the imperative of unconditionality.

To locate the "voice" of conscience in the silent interstices of discourse, as though it were a comma or semicolon in discursive consciousness, is to dislocate the delay. The *Unheimlich*, the uncanny, does not punctuate the for-itself, Dasein, because of a forgotten essence or an essential lethe, like a dire secret one cannot bring to awareness. Yet Heidegger's conscience behaves like a monster repressed by an authoritarian ego, a Minataur buried in the labyrinth of the psyche that demands periodic tribute. The enigma is how to lead a life without exhuming the grotesque, the abhorrent, the mutation, the monstrous, without waking the dictatorial, subterranean voice of the same. Thus marginalized, the Unheimlich, while "a threat to the lostness," threatens to devour the subject and leave it suspended in the belly of ontological care [*Sorge*].[3] Here, essence extends to every horizon and covers the same with total signification. Since the horizonal coincides with the horizontal and the same exhausts and is exhausted by the horizontal, Heidegger's essentialism is without a gap, a totalitarianism of the origin. Since the seamless essence of the horizontal is not really open to a disruptive verticality, its openness is only to more of the same, a dissimulation of the open. The danger posed when conscience calls for more of the same through the disguise of the subterranean remains unperceived because of engorgement by the same. That Heidegger's conscience exemplifies the "leveling by the same" and ignores Nietzsche's admonition concerning leveling demonstrates the perils of assigning conscience to being.

Since the same level permits no vertical, conscience is relegated to a kind of intraexistential event rather than a nonoccurrence that ruptures existence with its nonoccurring. Spoken from being to being, conscience does not derive authority from what is higher but from sleight of hand. Its uncanniness, discourse's resistance to it, is that of ventriloquism, of voice thrown to a place that is not its origin. Strange, preternatural trickery, conscience calls from below or above the horizontal but all the time dissembles and feigns. Its sound echoes with the real, but because it is always shadowed by its origin, it never escapes self-love and narcissism. Because conscience is made into a parlour game, the enigmatic is depleted of meaning and suspicion thrown on hierarchy and the hieratic.

The degenerateness of conscience in essentialism is a refracting of a refractory force, a dissipation of the disruptive, and therefore is deficient of the ethical. It is an ontological masquerade that denies the nonoriginary perturbation that is the real threat to its authoritarian designs. The scarred face of the other, the other's festering sores, destitution, prostitution, dismay, and deathly pallor, evoke a call in the subject that drains the ego of its imperialistic power. Since the guerilla attack is in retaliation of consciousness's insousiance, it reiterates the accusation that the other lodges against it. Inasmuch as the signification of the call is not exhausted by the summons, to call is also to command repayment of the loan. It is a stripping down of one's goods "unto death" in order to hand them over to the other, in whatever guise the other has taken. It is disempowerment at the hands of an anarchist whose other hand is on the grenade. It is no stately transaction of essence.

The enigma of conscience concerns the potentization of subjectivity by a recurrent disruption of the other. Since an enhanced energy level (like the spin of a gyroscope) allows the subject to remain face to face, positive, without negation, while in front of the disrupting force, the conscientious subject is able to be responsive in a nonevasive and direct manner. The science of conscience is that of exchange, and since the science is esoteric and initiatic, the subject is one who has been inducted into the mysterious transaction wherein the one appears in the other's place, healing the other's wounds through compassionate wisdom. Since to potentize requires violence and since the force of disruption itself violates the ego's autoeroticism, conscience too is a recurrence of violence, a holy war that pits subjectivity against itself. It is a war waged with disinterest. If not sham, the peace of conscience, like Heraclitean repose, is attainable only by way of self-struggle and the acceptance of self-struggle as initiatic. Through the violent rubbing of the one against the other, the other against the one, an energy center is established that is "relatively independent" of the surpassing energy of disruption. Combustion, ignition, and initiation are significations of the relative independence of conscience. They signify when the potentizable, the spark that can comprehend the incomprehensible, has become potent.

That conscience known as "the inner God" does not subtract from the enigma that is the deferral of the sign in the face of the signified. An ephemeral vagueness or a phenomenal sense of the exceptional that attends the enigma does not permit designation of itself other than as a hesitancy or delay in the designation of the same—like a mote of opacity crossing the solar disk. The very imperceptibility of the enigma does not render it any less enigmatic, any more than the constant presence of its absence does. That conscience responds on the basis of privative knowledge—knowledge that defers to the deferral—induces an aura of ironic ignorance. Socrates, who personified the potency of the subjective, was able sympathetically to induct others into the enigma since potentization is felt as seductive, as an eros not autoinfatuated, an eros desirous of the other. Socratic force, however potent, is never transparent or reflective if we take Socrates's self-humbling words that end the early dialogues at their face value: "I too am ignorant." Socratic force has the power of exchanging one for the other under cover of its ironic ignorance, as Alcibiades, who is initially the pursued, says at the end of the *Symposium*: "Our roles will seem to be reversed. . . . From this day, it shall be I who shall wait upon you, and you who will be waited upon by me."[4] The enigmatic exchange, which memory remembers only after it is underway, is potentized by a potentized subject, whose conscience is actualized to the degree that it accomplishes the inexplicable inexplicably without effort.

The hesitation that cannot be made present, the delay that speaks in the voice of the past, that is already over one's shadows when one goes to meet it: that is the signification of enigma. A quickened sensitivity and the subtle body of soma engender a time able to comprehend the time of nonpresence. Since the trope of a buried "organ" finds its credibility here, it can be said that conscience resides, if anywhere, in the inner body constituted by the energy relations of sensitivity. Addressed by the deferral of sign to signified, the enigmatic noncoincidence of meaning with itself, conscience speaks in reply in the voice of categorical disruption. Presiding inwardly as the "outer God" presides exteriorly, this "inner God" commands the imperative command of otherness, and the ego shucks its narcissistic skin to breathe in the command through its pores. The other in the one and the one in the other—starting positions now reversed—face each other, drawn seductively together by the exigence of exchange that takes precedence. Does the other's tortured body that mutely accuses me become my own accusation, and does my care for its wounds become that which names the other's enigmatic worth, that which takes precedence for both?

Do our hands touch the other's skin as our own, and do we each feel the for-itself violated by the other's responsiveness and obedience to what is higher? Does the call that strips me naked of pretentions and binds the other's wounds also denude the other of thoughts of injustice and the supremacy of the weak? Can our disjointed disharmonies each kindle the spark of otherness in the other, that we each become potentized and conscience-bound?

16

THE SURPASSING

Disruption is more surpassing than continuity because of what it lacks—an origin. Since a beginning is subject to boundary conditions and heteronomy, that which has never passed through the gates of existence knows a boundlessness and unconditionality in surpassing measure. A human subject is able through contact to be cognizant of a signification other than that of autonomy, one that is announced in an interval of retardation between sign and signified. Since autonomy involves the legislation of laws for oneself has sign and signified coincide, no delay is possible. Inasmuch as the zenith of autonomous subjectivity is, for Kant, a "pure spontaneity," the subject never escapes the beginning and its boundary conditions, even if the subject authorizes the moment. In autonomy is an obsession to safeguard its freedom whose obsessive expression is the continual free play of consciousness, losing and recovering itself in order to avoid abrupt disruption. In revealing the delay within signification, disruptive force shows the play as play and the author as player. Even though spontaneity instates an origin sui generis, origination itself bounds the subject heteronomously and limits its potential development to a horizontal increase of consciousness. Consciousness can become wary of the limit imposed by originary thought, and even intuit a possible ascent of awareness (in transcendental apperception), but it will always fall short of alteration and potentization. It will never surpass itself.

Since to surpass means to go beyond the past, disruption is surpassing because it belongs to an immemorial past. Of such a past, memory, records, and traditions are altogether lacking, not because of a limitation or defect in human subjectivity but because the past has never presented itself. The surpassing, therefore, is not subject to ontological examination, dialectical analysis, or discursive exegesis since it is or was never present and thereby slipped through the nets of representation. Of a past that never came into existence, the surpassing is deontological. If its signification is to be other than borrowed from ontology and essence's love of disclosure, deontological meaning, an infinitesmal deferral within the signs of essence, must evoke responsibility, obedience, and an unconditional liberation from the conditions of origination. A surpassing of the past, felt in the rupture of the same by force of otherness, is unruly, exceptional, and enigmatic. To welcome disruption requires a surpassing of an autoproductive consciousness empowered by self-interest—an alteration of consciousness. A past other than the represented past, the same past, the past of homage, pity, and forgiveness, must be borne in memory. To remember a time before time began is to be remembered to the surpassing. Subjectivity great enough to greet the disruptive other is remembered to the surpassing and thereby potentized.

The increase unto surpassing of subjectivity is an acceptation of anarchy, yet, paradoxically, a release from law giving is a release *to* responsibility. From the freedom of autonomy to the freedom of a categorical obedience, an increased patience more passive than passivity ceases to turn from the suffering other. The paradox that to relinguish the free play of consciousness, that to place it under a surpassing lawlessness, is to multiply responsibility exponentially is Dostoevsky's lament: "Instead of taking possession of men's freedom, Thou didst increase it and burdened the spiritual kingdom of mankind with its sufferings forever." Suffering not bound up in autoeroticism and self-love, that is not merely frustrated desire, is the suffering of otherness, the greater burden. This alien suffering, brought before the subject by the face of the other—even the other in oneself—calls forth a responsiveness beyond that of autonomy. Indicted by the other's accusation, I am called upon to exchange places with the other, to take on the suit of the other's suffering in exchange for my own, to suffer the other's suffering. The obligation to suffer an alien suffering, moreover, involves more than "gritting one's teeth," since an awareness of the transformative power of suffering must in all responsibility be communicated. To suffer is, therefore, to suffer the lack of ability to communicate the signification of suffering to the suffering other. Inasmuch as essential communication supposes order, an inflexible connection between sign and signified, and semiotic principles, communication of the ethical to the suffering other must throw everything overboard and without benefit of a beginning speak of a commandment that comes from no one.

The subject is center of an enigma that concerns a past that is discontinuous with the past once present. The enigma centers on *who* the subject is. The *who* involves the noncoincidence of essence and name, the fact that for subjectivity, the arche name *I* predates the essence of the subject and calls it into being—reversing the usual order whereby essence gives signs that designate a name that is itself. Inasmuch as *I* is the primordial utterance of disclosure, the first word *logos*, essence succeeds the arche name's exclamative *I am* in Fichtean fashion, like crystalization, concrescence, or hypostatization follows an original emanation. In the noncoincidence that makes subjectivity unique among beings, the unique of uniques, is the initial delay that indicates the ethical as well as the opportunity for initiation into the ethical. Since the *who* is gathered around a lag, a nonequivalance, an irresolution in its signification, it encompasses a difference, an otherness to being—as well as being the same that it is. Because the distance that separates these two points is unity divided by zero, subjectivity expresses the infinite in the moment it greets the disruptive other. Such expression expresses the uniqueness of the subject and consequently is remembered to the surpassing.

That the subject is a misfit in its genus and is not a concrete universal or generic individual also speaks to its contact with the surpassing. Not exhausted by its denomination, subjectivity remains on call, under an accusation that is more than nominal, and subjected to deontological signification that grants it no option but to answer. The ambiguity in subjectivity is not a freedom of meaning, but a rigorous obedience. The *who* is held to be responsible—regardless of whether it assents, and independent of any decision it makes. This responsibility, like the air awaiting an infant's first breath, attends the subject's birth and attended the birth of the human species. If I could speak this way, the responsibility is part of the "arrangement" by which the manifest is borrowed from the unmanifest. Although responsibility fills the subject like the ambient air, the *who* must be made cognizant of ambiguity, obedience, and the surpassing—that is, of contact with the alien in the one. Across an unbridgeable difference, a gap that can never be closed, one does infinitely more than mutually recognize the other (Hegel); one crosses over and takes the other's place. The memory that, pricked by disruptive force, remembers the *who* and the surpassing, is a call to become an initiate of the enigma of the ethical. Remembering the immemorial past, such memory sparks a revolution of anarchy, an unprincipled about-face by which I disinterestedly turn toward the other in need and trade places, mine for the other's, the other's for mine. Since the past that surpasses any past tense cannot be retained and is necessarily lost again, the subject is responsible for cultivating surpassing memory. To the extent that the *who* remembers itself, to that extent it has been initiated by and remembered to the surpassing.

Although intended for all, the ethical is, as implied by the term *initiatic*, attended only by some. The idea of the chosen itself is a contradiction since, if self-appointed, then the chosen are not chosen and, if chosen, they are designated by no one other than themselves. The enigmatic character of conscience does not quell anxieties of the chosenness of the chosen. At the same time, it is clear that the surpassing, while not presenting itself, makes its absence phenomenally felt. The surpassing does not entirely escape our human notice. Since the surpassing, in passing over, calls on humanity at large to make a mark on the doorpost, the opportunity of response is given to all. Although only the elect hear and take action, the election is not determined by conditions extrinsic to subjectivity. Nor is the election set once and for all, for all that is needed to join the ranks is, as Kant says, "a single unchangeable decision."[1] To leave the mark of conscience, moreover, is not an entitlement or the precursor to benefits, but the agreement to obey. Since the chosen are chosen to work, their attitude toward those who did not put up a mark and were passed over must differ from that of the *Exodus* account. To be put to death, mortally or spiritually, is not cause for those chosen to rejoice but to mourn in the homes of the mourners of the dead. The surpassing, the angel of death to insouciant humanity, of fear and trembling to those that hear, requires no homage or worship—though it is the universal and everlasting craving of humanity to find some entity to worship. Slipping into consciousness through the delay between the sign and the essence, the surpassing requires only that it be remembered. That conscience sparks action to take on the other's suffering and grant the other my ease is a clear acknowledgment of that memory.

The elect do not choose election for the reason that refusal but not choice is theirs. They are not elected by those whose election has already been assured because each one can give assurance only for itself. Nonetheless, without effort and striving, the conscious ego retains its supremacist assumptions, its xenophobia, its pretense of certitude, blocking memory of the surpassing. Since the ego is both enemy, infidel, barbarian, Egyptian, or anti-hero and the for-itself "ignorant of its own ignorance," the battering force of disruption must momentarily stop consciousness. In the response to the stoppage of autoproduction is revealed subjectivity's will to conscience. A willingness to alteration, the neutering of autoeroticism, and the violation of the autonomous person condition that response. Since response arises in the unruly fashion of disruption itself, cognition of the other is more unpredictable than matters of choice, spontaneity, and origination. The sole qualification to election is given by subjectivity itself. The statement that "Initiates initiate themselves," as a description of the ethical must be modified to take account of the guidance offered by the surpassing itself.

In subjectivity's potential for guidance lies its hope for potentization and conscience. What act allows the subject to fall back and follow the annunciation of ethical signification in the delay between sign and signified? What assumptions lead philosophy to a correct hermeutics of the phenomenology of deferral? A memory that lodges in one's throat and leaves the metal taste of remorse in one's mouth—that I have again forgotten what takes precedence and all that follows from it—initiates a turn toward hope, if not resisted. Errant and aimless, arriving in its own time, worked by its own will, such memory that is not a temporal accumulation, a treasure trove of information, is an epiphany of the surpassing, a remembrance of time more past than past. Although it explodes the perpetual peace of consciousness with an alien command to atonement, the commandment is uttered by the subject's lips in the subject's voice. The way in which one feels that imperative to relate to the other, to stand in the other's place while the other stands in mine, categorically surpasses all self-interest is by annihilation. Desire is surpassed, not by an act of will or willessness, but by the violence of an anarchical memory that reduces subjectivity to choiceless obedience. Inasmuch as the reduction is a potentization and refinement, the dross of ego is incinerated by combustion and a purified heart left as steward of remembrance. Since the repetition of desire is certainty, the recurrence of memory of the surpassing—the guide—is necessarily dubious, at risk, and without guarantee.

Like the other's curse given in return for my help, the disruption is a good that disguises itself. Spit in the face for my alms, shoved away for the helping hand, I am not allowed cheap self-approval. The recurrent discontinuity in autoproductive consciousness—the hoped-for guidance—causes a distaste for one's own ingratitude and the encrustations of self, in the place of which arises the willingness to serve. This alchemical exchange of the greater for the lesser, of worth for the worthless, lies at the heart of the enigma and the potentization of subjectivity. The lead of self-love is violated surpassingly to yield the gold of disinterest. In the midst of the night of egoistic autoproduction, one is visited and left an insomniac who atones for an unatonable forgetfulness with a compassionate heart. Since the wakefulness that has its seat in the soma is a sensitization to the suffering other, one reaches across the gap and changes places with him/her, thereby reenacting the mystery of exchange. Serving that mystery by recurring to a memory of the surpassing, one has incarnated—entrusted to the somatic logos—an inner power of disruption. That power is called "conscience."

POSTSCRIPT

THE MIGHTY

The discrepancy between effort and obedience—the ableness of the subject's effort and the force of obedience called forth from subjectivity—expresses a paradox. If effort measures a degree of responsiveness, then one is accountable for little. Then the secret and not-so-secret nihilism of Protagorean humanism that makes humanity the measure of all things would wear the amulet of truth and the self would truly be under its power. Unpredictable and impredicable rifts in the continuous play of consciousness that constitutes the world would be completely erased as marginal events, aberrations, synaptic misfirings. Their signification would be lost and, with it, the meaning of the gap between sign and signified would be erased and displaced "within the limits of reason alone."

The sole factor that prevents the tragic loss that afflicts humankind today is a sensitivity to the weakness and inadequacy of the subject in its present state. To put somnolence as measure of attainment is to cease to be wakened by the paradox of obedience. To hear a command—obedience in its root sense—that is commanded prior to any response, and yet response to which seals the very lips of the command, is to be wakened to the discrepancy I speak of. To hear a command that accuses one categorically of noncompliance and categorically obligates one to exchange places with the accuser—the other—is to measure one's human capability against that of the mighty. It is to bow one's autonomy before the altar of the mighty and with the patience of passivity set aside denial and insousiance in order to embrace that which takes precedence.

The sacrifice of the ego's dream of transparency, our Cartesian birthright, initiates movement in a consciousness that heretofore had been fixed. The combustion of transparency and the simultaneous darkening of the mind's eye (the lumen naturale) opens the subject to the soma, sensitivity, and the subtle body, whose appearances are heralded by disruption. Disruption is the flame at the altar of the mighty, whose might recurrently commands cessation and resurrection—cessation of self-enclosure and resurrection of the shared body of humanity. In commanding an exchange, the imperative voice commands not only that my body take the place of the other's (and the other's, mine), but also that both bodies be uplifted, refined, and purified of the suffering of separateness. To heal the pain of noncontinguity and to be touched by the touch of the mighty, to be remembered by a memory of the surpassing, is to be re-membered (as a part to a whole) to the singularity of purpose of humanity. Being without origin, the memory of humanity's purpose occasionally arouses subjects from the nightmare of separateness and wakes the shared body of humanity to action. It is then, in this stirring of conscience, that attainment to the ethical is possible.

The subject's inability to engage in conscientious action, even on the level of praxis, when juxtaposed with the absolute obedience owed the mighty, reiterates the paradox. Since might is intensity, the mighty is an infinite intensification of subjective responsiveness, a perfection of the libation implied in a response. Love of the mighty, the surpassing in command, is the name of praxis itself. "Love the Lord thy God with all thy heart, with all thy soul, and with all thy might."

Conversely, the enigmatic bending of the infinite that touches finite curvature of humanity at every point is mercy. That the discrepancy between response and obligation is no cause for punishment, that it is erased by forgiveness at each recurrence to the other, is confirmed by the fact that praxis is mightier than forgetfulness. Might recurs to disrupt the pretension of weakness—even the warp of weakness that is evil—and dispel the clouds of inadequacy. From a fumbling, indifferent, inarticulate saying of effort to a forceful, direct, eloquent pronouncement, might touches the subject and confers its enabling grace. That which is other than consciousness uplifts the heart with hope and opens the way toward initiation. One reaches across the difference to the other whose face is worn with pain and whose heart turns away in humiliation. Although difference remains, in that gesture, love restores one to a memory of human destiny that has awaited humanity *and* remembers one to the surpassing. In that spirit, one touching the other is no different than the other being touched by the surpassing.

That we are lacking in the very breath that sustains us—love—and must, therefore, earn it is the enigma. The work is a matter of intensification. To gather a force that disrupts the dispersed self of autoeroticism, the consciousness of the same, one comes to a stop. Accepting inadequacy, a patience more constant than a consequence places itself under authority of what is higher. Although this nonaction is no more potent than the disrupted impotency, difference enlists difference and the merciful intercession of a force intercedes whose precedence is without argument. Disposed to obey, one listens to a commandment uttered by one's own lips and is potentized in the way that hearing truth from one's own utterances potentizes. From intensity to intensity, might to might, one moves by quanta, discontinuously, nondialectically, toward an ableness to respond to the exigence of a situation.

The subject who bows before the might of the other—"the mighty one, blessed be he!"—participates in a might other than his/her own. Since it is not a force that can be gesturally appropriated, it is without meaning in the realm of being. Strictly speaking, we cannot say that disruptive might *is* or *is not*, *is* and *is not*, or even neither *is* nor *is not*. The ontological silence regarding the question of the mighty's being is antinomous. It signifies, like the infinitesmal delay between an ontological sign and the essence it signifies, the signification of the ethical, that is, the other-than-being. That delay is nothing other than the compassionate heart's stumbling articulation in the face of the mighty. The bow—a bodily rendition of delay—repeats the paradox. Since by lowering itself, subjectivity comes into contact with that which lies above the subject, it places itself under the laws governing exchange. To the degree possible, the subject changes places with the force of might, as it were, putting on its clothes, feeling its pain. Bowing, one feels the mighty's response to the exigence of creation, its need for enlightenment. In the bow, the paradox expresses how subordination becomes might without recourse to the gesture of meaning.

The bow allows the subject to become *as though* mighty. Although the subject is the noncoincidence of effort and might, this very discrepancy is a disruptive force that pushes effort beyond effort toward the root meaning, which transcends strength in the direction of love. In the face of the other whose exigence speaks for all creatures, might precipitates a disrobing of interest and a disinterested approach to the fact of obligation. The thick walls of separateness having crumbled before the superior strength of the mighty, the naked subject is free to trade places with beggar, leper, even the condemned of the gas chamber, because all signs that signify specialness have also been expunged. From beyond, the mighty has passed over and the sign of salvation (postscripted on every door of the chosen) signifies acceptation as a worker in the furtherance of life.

NOTES

CHAPTER 1. INSTRUMENTS

1. "De Memoria et Reminiscentia," 450 b 17–19, tr. J. I. Beare, in *The Basic Works of Aristotle,* ed. Richard McKeon (New York: Random House, 1941).

2. Ibid., 449b 5–8.

3. John Locke, *An Essay Concerning Human Understanding,* ed. Maurice Cranston (New York: Macmillan, 1965), II.x, p. 95.

4. John Locke, "An Essay Concerning the True Original, Extent, and End of Civil Government," in *The English Philosophers from Bacon to Mill,* ed. Edwin A. Burtt (New York: Random House, 1939), p. 413.

5. René Descartes, "Discourse on the Method," in *Descartes: Philosophical Writings,* trans. and ed. by Elizabeth Anscombe and Peter Geach (London: Nelson, 1964), p. 38.

6. "Concerning Civil Government," in *The English Philosophers from Bacon to Mill,* ed. Edwin A. Burtt, p. 404.

7. Ibid.

8. Sigmund Freud, *Psychopathology of Everyday Life,* trans. A. A. Brill (New York: New American Library, 1951), p. 7.

9. This and related themes are thoroughly explored by Luce Irigaray. Cf. her *Speculum of the Other Woman,* trans. Gillian C. Gill (Ithaca, N.Y.: Cornell University Press, 1985).

10. Locke, *An Essay Concerning Human Understanding,* III.1, p. 229.

11. Ibid., II.9, p. 267.

12. Ibid.

13. Thomas Hobbes, "Leviathan: or the Matter, Form, and Power of a Commonwealth Ecclesiastical and Civil," in *The English Philosophers from Bacon to Mill,* ed. Edwin A. Burtt (New York: Random House, 1939), p. 133.

14. David Hume, *An Inquiry Concerning Human Understanding,* ed. Charles W. Hendel (New York: Liberal Arts Press, 1955), pp. 29–30, my italics.

15. Ibid., p. 28.

16. Ibid., p. 26.

17. Ibid., p. 27.

CHAPTER 2. USAGES

1. Friedrich Nietzsche, *The Genealogy of Morals,* trans. Francis Golffing (New York: Doubleday, 1956), p. 189.

2. Ibid.

3. Hume, *An Inquiry Concerning Human Understanding,* p. 26.

4. Francis Bacon, "Novum Organum," in *The English Philosohers from Bacon to Mill,* ed. Edwin A. Burtt (New York: Random House, 1939), section xli, p. 34.

5. Locke, *An Essay Concerning Human Understanding,* II.1, p. 63.

6. Ibid., p. 64.

7. David Hume, *A Treatise of Human Nature,* ed. L. A. Selby-Bigge (Oxford: The Clarendon Press, 1888), I.1.2, p. 21.

8. Ibid., p. 8.

9. Hume, *An Inquiry Concerning Human Understanding,* p. 30.

10. Dorion Cairns, *Conversations with Husserl and Fink,* ed., The Husserl Archives, *Phaenomenologica* 50 (The Hague: Martinus Nijhoff, 1973), passim.

11. Psalm 114. 16; compare, Locke, *An Essay Concerning Civil Government,* p. 413.

12. Immanuel Kant, *Critique of Pure Reason,* trans. Norman Kemp Smith (London: Macmillan, 1950), A167–B209.

13. Ibid.

14. Ibid.

15. Ibid., A168–B210.

16. Ibid., A143–B182.

17. Ibid., B131.

18. Ibid., B134.

19. *Maitri Upanisad* 6:34, in *The Thirteen Principal Upanishads,* trans. Robert Ernest Hume (New York: Oxford University Press, 1921).

20. Locke, *An Essay Concerning Human Understanding,* III.9, p. 353.

21. Ibid., II.xiii; p. 113.

22. Hume, *An Inquiry Concerning Human Understanding,* p. 27.

23. Kant, *Critique of Pure Reason,* A150–B197.

CHAPTER 3. HUSSERL AND INTERNAL TIME-CONSCIOUSNESS

1. Edmund Husserl, *The Phenomenology of Internal Time-Consciousness,* ed. Martin Heidegger, trans. James S. Churchill (Bloomington: Indiana University Press, 1964), p. 50.
2. Ibid.
3. Ibid.
4. Ibid., p. 51.
5. 450b 17–19, in McKeon, *Basic Works of Aristotle.*
6. Hume, *A Treatise of Human Nature,* I.1.iv.
7. Husserl, *The Phenomenology of Internal Time-Consciousness,* p. 53.
8. Ibid., p. 61.
9. Ibid., p. 50

CHAPTER 4. TOWARD A SOMATIC CRITIQUE OF RETENTIVITY

1. Gabriel Marcel, *The Mystery of Being,* vol. 1, *Reflection and Mystery,* trans. G. S. Fraser (South Bend: Gateway, 1950), pp. 77–78.
2. Ibid., p. 78.
3. Ibid., p. 79.
4. Hobbes, "Leviathan," in *The English Philosophers from Bacon to Mill,* p. 161.

CHAPTER 5. THE BETWEENNESS OF THE SOMATIC FIELD

1. See Reiner Schurmann, *Meister Eckhart: Mystic and Philosopher* (Bloomington: Indiana University Press, 1978), p. 144.
2. Cairns, *Conversations with Husserl and Fink,* pp. 78–79.
3. Ibid., p. 14.
4. Ibid., p. 78.
5. Ibid., p. 79.
6. Gabriel Marcel, *Being and Having,* trans. Katherine Farrer (New York: Harper and Row, 1965), p. 13.
7. "Physics," trans. R. P. Hardie and R. K. Gaye, in *McKeon, The Basic Works of Aristotle,* 250b.11–13.
8. *A Treatise of Human Nature,* I.II.iii, p. 32.

9. Ibid.

10. *Being and Having,* p. 11.

11. Cairns, *Conversations with Husserl and Fink,* p. 2.

12. *Metaphysical Journal,* trans. Bernard Wall (Chicago: Regnery, 1952), p. 297; cf. *Creative Fidelity,* trans. Robert Rosthal (New York: Farrar, Straus, 1964), p. 25.

13. Proclus, *Treatise on the Hieratic Art of the Greeks,* cited in Henry Corbin, *Creative Imagination in the Sufism of Ibn 'Arabi,* trans. Ralph Manheim (Princeton, N.J.: Princeton University Press, 1969), p. 105.

14. Kant, *Critique of Pure Reason,* B5.

CHAPTER 7. THE INTERVAL

1. John Burnet, *Early Greak Philosophy* (New York: Meridian Books, 1957), fr. 35, 36, pp. 211–212. Cf. G. S. Kirk and J. E. Raven, *The Presocratic Philosophers* (Cambridge: Cambridge University Press, 1957), fr. 464, pp. 346–347: "When Strife had reached to the lowest depth of the whirl and Love was in the middle of the eddy, under her do all these things come together so as to be one, not all at once but congregating each from different directions at their will. And as they came together Strife began to move outwards to the circumference. . . . And in proportion as it was ever running forth outwards, so a gentle immortal stream of blameless Love was ever coming in."

2. Kirk and Raven, *The Presocratic Philosophers,* fr. 430, p. 331.

3. Edmund Husserl, *Ideas: General Introduction to Pure Phenomenology,* trans. W. B. Boyce Gibson (New York: Macmillan, 1962), p. 99.

4. Ibid., p. 100.

CHAPTER 8. OBJECTIVITY AND MEANING

1. Locke, *An Essay Concerning Human Understanding,* III.1, p. 229.

2. *Meditations,* in Anscombe and Geach, *Philosophical Writings,* p. 63.

3. Recent work in logical syntax emphasizes Leibniz's law of the indiscernibility of identicals. For example, "given a true statement of identity, one of its two terms may be substituted for

the other in any true statement and the result will be true." Willard Van Orman Quine, *From a Logical Point of View* (New York: Harper and Row, 1953), p. 139.

4. John Locke, *An Essay Concerning Human Understanding,* III.6, p 253.

5. Ibid., III.6., p. 250.

6. *Paracelsus: Selected Writings,* ed. Jolande Jacobi (Princeton, N.J.: Princeton University Press, 1951), p. 122.

7. Ibid., pp. 121–122.

CHAPTER 9. SYMPATHY AND THE PLIGHT OF THE SELF

1. Martin Heidegger, *On Time and Being,* trans. Joan Stambaugh (New York: Harper and Row, 1972), p. 19.

2. Jacobi, *Paracelsus, Selected Writings,* p. 121.

3. Ibid., p. 123.

4. Ibid., p. 121.

CHAPTER 10. "BECOMING SIMILAR"

1. *De Anima* 1.2, 404b 17, in *The Basic Works of Aristotle,* ed. Richard McKeon, trans. J. A. Smith (New York: Random House, 1941); Kirk and Raven, *The Presocratic Philosophers,* p. 343. Cf. Aristotle, *Metaphysics* IV: 1000b 6.

2. Jacobi, *Paracelsus, Selected Writings,* pp. 122–123.

3. Cited in Reiner Schurmann, *Meister Eckhart: Mystic and Philosopher* (Bloomington: Indiana University Press, 1978), p. 94.

4. Theophrastus, *de sensu;* cited by Kirk and Raven, *The Presocratic Philosohers,* p. 343.

5. *Meditations,* in Anscombe and Geach, ed., *Philosophical Writings,* p, 113.

6. Ibid., p. 70.

7. Cited in Schurmann, *Meister Eckhart,* p. 144.

8. Jacobi, *Paracelsus, Selected Writings,* p. 128.

CHAPTER 11. NONDISCLOSURE

1. Kant, *Critique of Pure Reason,* B274.

2. Plato, *Symposium* 215d, trans. Michael Joyce, in *Collected Dialogues,* ed. Hamilton and Cairns.

3. *Passions of the Soul* II, xlv; in Anscombe and Geach, ed., *Philosophical Writings,* p. 361.

4. Kant, *Critique of Pure Reason,* A297–B353.

5. Heidegger, *On Time and Being,* p. 21.

6. Heidegger, *Parmenides,* cited by Joan Stambaugh, *The Finitude of Being* (Albany: State University of New York Press, 1992) p. 43.

7. Benedict de Spinoza, *The Ethics,* trans. R. H. M. Elwes (New York: Dover, 1955), IV. prop. 39, p. 215.

CHAPTER 12. INITIATION

1. Heidegger, *On Time and Being,* p. 19.

2. Kant, *Critique of Pure Reason,* A107.

3. Plato, *Symposium* 213c, in *The Collected Dialogues of Plato,* ed. Hamilton and Cairns.

CHAPTER 13. SUFFERING AND THE PASSIVITY OF THE SUBJECT

1. "Desire is the actual essence of man insofar as it is conceived, as determined to a particular activity by some given modification of itself." Spinoza, *Ethics* III, definition 1, p. 173.

2. *Meister Eckhart,* trans. Raymond B. Blakney (New York: Harper and Row, 1941), p. 157.

3. Kant, *Critique of Pure Reason* A497–B525.

CHAPTER 14. EFFORT AND PRAXIS

1. Kant, *The Moral Law,* trans. H. J. Paton (London: Hutchinson University Library, 1948), p. 61.

2. Ibid., p. 99.

3. "About Disinterest," in *Meister Eckhart,* trans. Raymond B. Blakney, p. 88.

CHAPTER 15. CONSCIENCE

1. *The Doctrine of Virtue,* trans. Mary J. Gregor (New York: Harper and Row, 1964), pp. 60–61.

2. Heidegger, *Being and Time,* trans. John Macquarrie and Edward Robinson (New York: Harper and Row, 1962), H273, p. 318.

3. Ibid., H277, p. 322.

4. *Symposium* 135d, in *Collected Dialogues,* ed. Hamilton and Cairns.

CHAPTER 16. THE SURPASSING

1. *Religion Within the Limits of Reason Alone,* trans. Theodore M. Greene and Hoyt H. Hudson (New York: Harper and Row, 1960), p. 43.

BIBLIOGRAPHY

Adams, George, *Physical and Ethereal Spaces.* London: Rudolf Steiner Press, 1965.

Anscombe, Elizabeth, and Peter Geach, trans. and ed., *Descartes: Philosophical Writings.* London: Nelson, 1964.

Blakney, Raymond B., trans., *Meister Eckhart.* New York: Harper and Row, 1941.

Burtt, Edwin A., ed. *The English Philosophers from Bacon to Mill.* New York: Random House, 1939.

Cairns, Dorion, *Conversations with Husserl and Fink,* ed. The Husserl Archives, *Phaenomenologica* 66. The Hague: Martinus Nijhoff, 1976.

Corbin, Henry, *Creative Imagination in the Sufism of Ibn 'Arabi,* trans. Ralph Manheim. Princeton, N.J.: Princeton University Press, 1969.

Derrida, Jacques, *Memoires of the Blind,* trans. Pascale-Anne Brault and Micahel Nass. Chicago: University of Chicago Press, 1993.

Descartes, René, *Descartes: Philosophical Writings,* trans. and ed. Elizabeth Anscombe and Peter Geach. London: Nelson, 1964.

Eckhart, *Meister Eckhart,* trans. Raymond Bernard Blakney. New York: Harper and Row, 1941.

Foucault, Michel. *The Order of Things.* New York: Random House, 1970.

Freud, Sigmund, *Psychopathology of Everyday Life,* trans. A. A. Brill. New York: New American Library, 1951.

Hamilton, Edith, and Huntington Cairns, eds., *The Collected Dialogues of Plato.* Princeton, N.J.: Princeton University Press, 1961.

Heidegger, Martin, *Being and Time,* trans. John Macquarrie and Edward Robinson. New York: Harper and Row, 1962.

———. *On Time and Being,* trans. Joan Stambaugh. New York: Harper and Row, 1972.

Hendel, Charles W., ed. *An Inquiry Concerning Human Understanding.* New York: Liberal Arts Press, 1955.

Hobbes, Thomas, "Leviathan," in *The English Philosophers from*

Bacon to Mill, ed. Edwin A. Burtt. New York: Random House, 1939.

Hume, David, *An Inquiry Concerning Human Understanding*, ed. Charles W. Hendel. New York: Liberal Arts Press, 1955.

———, *A Treatise of Human Nature*, ed. L. A. Selby-Bigge. Oxford: Clarendon Press, 1888.

Husserl, Edmund, *Ideas: General Introduction to Pure Phenomenology*, trans. W. B. Boyce Gibson. New York: Macmillan, 1962.

———, *The Phenomenology of Internal Time-Consciousness*, ed. Martin Heidegger, trans. James S. Churchill. Bloomington: Indiana University Press, 1964.

Irigaray, Luce, *Speculum of the Other Woman*, trans. Gillian C. Gill. Ithaca, N.Y.: Cornell University Press, 1985.

Jacobi, Jolande, ed., *Paracelsus: Selected Writings*, trans. Norbert Guterman. Princeton, N.J.: Princeton University Press, 1951.

Kant, Immanuel, *Critique of Pure Reason*, trans. Norman Kemp Smith. London: Macmillan, 1950.

———, *The Moral Law*, trans. H. J. Paton. London: Hutchinson Home Library, 1948.

———, *The Doctrine of Virtue*, trans. Mary Gregor. New York: Harper and Row, 1964.

Kirk, G. S., and J. E. Raven, *The Presocratic Philosophers*. Cambridge: Cambridge University Press, 1957.

Levinas, Emmanuel, *Totality and Infinity*, trans. Alphonso Lingis. Pittsburgh: Duquesne University Press, 1969.

________, "Bad Conscience and the Inexorable," in *Face to Face with Levinas*, ed. Richard A. Cohen. Albany, State University of New York Press, 1986, pp. 35-41.

Locke, John, *An Essay Concerning the True Original, Extent, and End of Civil Government*, in *The English Philosophers from Bacon to Mill*, ed. Edwin A. Burtt. New York: Random House, 1939.

———, *An Essay Concerning Human Understanding*, ed. Maurice Cranston. New York: Macmillan, 1965.

Marcel, Gabriel, *Mystery of Being*, vol. 1, trans. G. S. Fraser. South Bend, Ind.: Gateway, 1950.

________, *Being and Having*, trans. Katherine Fraser. New York: Harper and Row, 1965.

McKeon, Richard, ed., *The Basic Works of Aristotle*. New York: Random House, 1941.

Paracelsus: Selected Writings, Jolande Jacobi, ed., Norbert Guterman, trans. Princeton, N.J.: Princeton University Prtess, 1951.

Quine, Willard Van Orman, *Word and Object*. Cambridge, MA: MIT Press, 1960.

Russell, Bertrand, *Logic and Knowledge*. London: Allen & Unwin, 1958.

Sartre, Jean-Paul, *Being and Nothingness: An Essay on Phenomenological Ontology*, trans. Hazel Barnes. New York: Philosophical Library, 1956.

Schurmann, Reiner, *Meister Echkart: Mystic and Philosopher*. Bloomington: Indiana University Press, 1978.

de Spinoza, Benedict, *The Ethics*, in *The Chief Works of Benedict de Spinoza*, trans. R. H. M. Elwes. New York: Dover, 1955.

Stambaugh, Joan, *The Finitude of Being*. Albany: State University of New York Press, 1992.

INDEX

A
Ablauf, 44, 57, 64, 80
Abschattung, 53, 54
Action, 18; chosen course of, 129; deviation of, 129; displaced, 49; moral, 62; of percipience, 61; reciprocity of, 17; and syllogism, 134
Advaita Vedanta, 30–31
Affection, 4
Affectivity, 7, 48
Alcibiades, 111, 151
Anarchaic: force, ix, 80; limits, 66; power, 141
Anarchaic function, 46; and perception, 34; and retention, 21
Anarchy, 94, 106, 154, 156
Angst, 133
Antahkarana, 30
Arche name *I,* 29, 30, 64, 66, 75, 93, 101, 130, 131, 132, 138, 148; disclosure of, 66; as disruptor, 29; meaningfulness in, 96; and subjectivity, 67; utterance of, 96, 109, 129
Aristotle, 4, 40, 42. 55, 56, 103, 106, 134
Autonomy, 125, 134; contradiction of, 121; dream of, 119; elevation of, 147; transparency of, 134
Autoproduction, 84, 85, 88, 89, 92, 112, 138, 142, 158
Avoidance, 9
Awareness: articulation of, 29; disruption of, ix; existential, 27, 28, 29, 64, 65; gathering of, 66; of impressions, 15; of inner speech, 21; levels of, 21; modes of, 1; moments of, 25; of obligation, 147; of reality, 7; somatic, xi, 1, 22, 24, 25, 27, 28, 29, 51, 53, 56, 59–60, 64, 74; and sympathy, xiii; unfolding of, 17; unproductivity in, 15

B
Being: beyond, 125; circle of, 113; concealment of, 112; and consciousness, vii, 125; deliverance of, 95; disclosing, 105; and discourse, ix; disruption of, 116; ease of, 132; human, 40; measure of, 122; meeting, 49; negation of, 56; of nomenclature, 91; and objectivity, 91; quantification of, 91; revelations of, 125; satisfaction with, 116; sleep of, ix; temporalization of, 40; in time, 27, 29, 34; transparent horizon of, vii; without origin, 160
Blank, 18; avoidance of, 5; danger in, 3; existence of, 14; filling in, 9; impress of, 10; and intellect, 6; and language, 10; and memory, 21; of mind, 3–10, 9; neutralization of, 19; power of, 13; role in discourse, 3; threat to intellect, 4
Body: earth, 61; gross, 105; life, 58; movement of, 56; praxis, xi; shared, 160; subtle, xi, 61, 105, 160
Bondage, 30
Bracketing, 81, 83, 84–85; of natural attitude, 108; of ontology, vii

C
Camus, Albert, 123
Catharsis, 19, 48

Cerberus, 81
Coenesthesis, 53
Communication: crux of, 105; of the ethical, 155; of meaning, 47; public, 29; with real constitution of things, 92; of thought, 12
Conflict: with logos, 107; in nature, 7; resolution of, 7
Conscience, x–xi, 145–152; authority of, 149; degenerateness of, 150; development of, xi; enigma of, 147, 150; in essentialism, 150; and exchange, 150; mark of, 156; power of, 158; privation of, 147; and responsibility, 147; within subjectivity, 108; voice of, 149
Consciousness, 160; acquisition of movement in, 96; and agreement, 83; anarchaic limits of, 66; autoproduction of, 112, 138, 142, 158; aversion to disruption, vii; avoidance in, 9; awareness of meaning in, 104; based on retention, 7; and being, vii, 125; birth of, 67; breaking into, xi; calm of, viii; categories in, 92; conditions of production of, vii; death of, 15; demands on, 63; destabilization of, 106; destiny of, 81; and difference, 55, 105; discourse of, ix; disruptive likeness of, 108; dissatisfaction in, 131; dissolution of, 13; egocentrism of, 106; essentialism in, xiv; Euclidean, 74; in exchange, 48; fear of immediacy, 48; flow of, 46; fractured, 94; freedom of, ix–x, 65; and the gaze, 9; hegemony of, 105; higher levels of, xiv; human, 43, 81; image of, 107, 108; of immediacy, 15; of impressions, 15, 17, 42; intentionality of, 142; inversion of, 14; lack of sleep in, 87; and loss, 55; memory in, xii; in movement, 58, 63, 159; natural state of, 84; obedience of, 109; objectifying, 84–85; optical, 74; original, 43, 66, 121; of the other, xi; percipient, 60, 94; and persistance in time, 81; as principle of essence, 91; production of, 46; protection from the other, 75; recovery of, vii; recurrence in somatic logos, 99; as recurrence of violence, 150; replication of, 89–90; representational, 16, 92; responsibility of, 119; retentional, 42, 63, 81; rupture of, xii; self-constituting, 35, 51; self-creation of, 106; self-identical, 43; self-legislating, vii; self-love of, 84–85; self-making, 47; sense of place in, 62; somatic, 34; speaking of speaking in, 109; speech to, 108; storytelling character of, 51; and subjectivity, 57, 65; subjunctive, 89; and submission, 66; and sympathy, 62, 104; time, 39–44; tolerance for disruption, ix; transformative, 58; void in, 81; vulnerability of, 75
Consciousness, altered, vii, 58, 74, 81, 92; causes of, 35; and difference, 96; integrity of, 84; by movement, 57; perception in, 52, 60; and somatic memory, 59; and sympathy, xiii; time in, 61; volition in, 103
Consciousness, object, 1, 7, 89; and blankness, 10; direction of, 15; enervation of, 18; point of erasure in, 9; power of, 19; problem-solving in, 45; and rep-

etition, 13; and sameness, 23; self-mastery of, 44
Consequentialism, 123
Consistency, 26
Continuity, 41, 42; of continuity, 43; of exchange, 64; love of, 92; preservation of, 80; renewal of, 44; in space, 58; temporal, 58, 119
Contraction, 35
Correspondence, 93, 94; and mutuality, 124; text of, 99; in text of likeness, 103

D

Dasein, 75, 82, 83, 88, 114, 149
Death: by death, 49; meaning of, 84–85; and remembrance, 113
De Memoria et Reminiscentia (Aristotle), 42
Descartes, René, 6, 27, 55, 82, 89, 99, 105, 111, 112, 130
Despair, ix
Difference: abolishment of, 28; acceptance of, 117; annulment by the gaze, 16; appearance of, 96; and consciousness, 55, 105; contingency of likeness in, 105; degree of, 21; and disruption, 60, 130; distance without, 28; energy, 61; and equality, 21, 92; knowing of, 60; lack of reason in, 17; and object consciousness, 23; and perception, 22; temporalization of, 57, 75, 82, 83
Disclosure: and discourse, 112; and essence, 111, 114; limiting factor of, 111; measurement of, 112; of resistance, 121; responsibility of, 124–125; sadness in, 115
Discourse: accidental, 12; and being, ix; blank in, 3; breaks in, ix; of consciousness, ix; contexts of, 11; and disclosure, 112; and human acts, vii; and imagination, 75; and inner speech, 12; and language, 12; moral, 133; possession of, 12; resiliance of, ix; semantic intent of, 12; silent, 149; thematizing of, 81; universe of, 100
Disinterest, 139, 140
Displacement, 9, 13
Disruption, 68; action of, 21; adaptation to, 141; as anarchaic creation, 96; anticipating, 19; of being, 116; and bracketing, vii; command of, viii, 119; creation of contact in, 57; denial of, 28, 105; and devaluation, vii; and difference, 130; disarming of, 19; disavowal of, 46; discontinuous character of, vii; by discursive thought, 112; and disintegration, vii; of the disruption, 126; dissipation of, 150; energy emission in, 46; and essence, 125; fear of, ix, 48, 59, 82, 131; of human acts, vii; incomprehension in, 130; inner, 64, 158; intermittancy of, 29; lack in, 153; made undisruptive, 112; marginalization of, 81; meaning of, 29; of memory, 35, 37; of the ongoing, 91; origin of, 153; and pathology, 48; pathos of, 17; of percipience, 64; precipitation of, xii; protection from, 30, 35; reflection in, 45; result of, 46; to sensation, 26, 29; signification of, xii; and social justice, 145; sublimation of, 48; and substitution, 104; of suffering, 101, 129; as surpassing, 153–158; termination, 48; threat of, xi; tolerance of consciousness for,

Disruption *(continued)*
ix; of tradition, xii, xiii; and transparency, 28; utility of, 46; victimization by, 116; vigilance toward, 1
Distraction, 21
Domination, 6
Dostoevsky, Fyodor, ix, 145, 154
Dreams, 87

E

Eckhart, Meister, 52, 104, 106, 107, 132, 140
Ego: and anger, 112; authoritarianism of, 145; autoeroticism of, 150; autonomous, 126; destabilization of, 145; dream of transparency, 159; extinguishing, 126; identification of, 134; obligations of, 81; shrinking, 65; and subjectivity, 93; subordination to soma, 65
Empedocles, 79, 81, 103, 105, 106
Empiricism, 40
Energy: animating, 60; circulation of, 48, 55; configurations of, 25, 79; crisis in, 17; difference, 61; discharge of, 18; dispersal of, 15; emission in disruption, 46; exchange of, 7; loss of, 72; movement of, 25; somatic, 27, 49, 53, 61
Enigma: of conscience, 147, 150; of the ethical, 145; of *Nichtdasein*, 132; of obedience, x; between sign and signified, 146
Epicureanism, xiii
Ereignis, 95, 113, 122
Eris, 79, 80, 83, 106, 109
Eros, 9, 18, 79, 80, 106
Essay Concerning Human Understanding (Locke), 4
Essence: community of, 92; correspondence in, 104; demand of subjectivity on, 112; and desire, 131; and disclosure, 99, 111, 114; and disruption, 125; as dynamis, 95; as the essential, 95; expression of, 125; goodness of, 97; and image, 108; and inequality, 97; initiation of, 96, 124; knowledge of, 98; language of, 97; and meaning, 93, 95; neglect of, 99; noncoincidence of, 133; overruled by equality, 92; presence, 104; as principle of consciousness, 91; and representation, 92; revelation of, 96; secret vow of, 98, 104; self-referential, 91; signification by, 112, 148; speech of, 98; and subjectivity, 95, 98, 125; and sympathy, 97, 103
Essentialism, xiv, 92, 93, 95, 99, 100, 103, 104, 114, 116, 122, 131, 133, 149, 150
Eternalism, xiii
Ethics: attainment of, 160; basis of, ix; denial of, xiii; of despair, ix; dispositional theory of, 4; of distress, 21; enigma of, 145; expression of, xiii; forceful advent of, x; initiation of, viii–ix, 123; openness of, 116; risk in, viii; of separateness, 49, 57, 65; of sorcery, 22; in subjectivity, 130; subject of, 133; and suffering, 101, 131; undoing in, viii
Euclid, 32, 72
Exchange: and conscience, 150; consciousness in, 48; continuity of, 64; cost of, 117; defining, 63; of energy, 7; intellectual, 5; lack in sleep, 117; mystery of, x, xii, 158; and perception, 60; of places, 159; rules of, 7
Existence: and accusation, 91; awareness of, 28; of the blank,

14; knowledge of, 31; noncoincidence of, 133; of perception, 28; of thought, xiv, 19
Experience: objects of, 33; possibility of, 33

F
Fantasy, 48
Fear: of discontinuity, 35, 65, 138; of disruption, ix, 48, 59, 82, 83, 131; of exposure, 4; of immediacy, 48; nature of, 44; of nonexistence, 35; of poverty, 5–6; of stoppage, 61
Foreknowledge, 33, 41
"Forgetting of Proper Names" (Freud), 9
Freedom: of consciousness, 65; limits of, 65; perfect, 7; safeguarding, vii
Freud, Sigmund, 9

G
Gap: in continuity of exchange, 64, 158; in memory, 3; in space, 28; in subjectivity, viii
the Gaze: afterimage in, 42; annulment of difference by, 16; averting, 42; and consciousness, 9; constricting communication, 47; expanding vision of, 6; hegemony of, 33; illumination by, 31; at infinity, 42; inner, 9; limits of, 32; loss of, 27, 32; misplay of, 55; position of, 84–85; and retention, 16; of retention, 9, 54; of retentivity, 24, 48; rigidity of, 6; and sight, 52; on the soma, 47; teleology of, 4; vulnerability in, 4
The Genealogy of Morals (Nietzsche), 21
Geocentrism, 69
Geometry: Euclidean, 33, 69, 71, 72; optical, 32, 71; plane in, 33, 69, 70, 71; point in, 33, 69, 70, 71; projective, 33, 69–74; space of, 28; synthetic, 33, 69; visual, 31–33
Geometry (Euclid), 32

H
Hamlet, 80
Hegel, Georg, 156
Heidegger, Martin, ix, 95, 113, 124, 148, 149
Herabsinken, 35, 40, 41*fig*
Heraclitus, 80
Hinabsinken, 60, 80, 84–85
Hobbes, Thomas, 13, 40, 66
Hume, David, 1, 13, 14, 15, 16, 17, 21, 22, 23, 24, 28–29, 33, 43, 57, 60, 115, 125
Husserl, Edmund, vii, xi, xiii, 25, 35, 39–44, 51, 53, 59, 81, 84
Hyletic flow, xi, 63, 93, 94, 104

I
Ideas: derivation of, 22, 33; dormancy in, 4; exclusiveness of, 14; fixation of, 4; holding on to, 87; and impression, 16; proto, 15; ready for viewing, 6
Identity: basis of, 112; denial of, 29; emergence of, 53; human, 6–7; real, 29; self, 61, 84
Idleness, 11
Ignorance, perfect, 5, 11, 87
Imagination, 13; active, 104; and discourse, 75; and memory, 13, 42; and percipience, 104; productive, 43, 56, 104; recombinant, 106; reproductive, 40, 87; ruination of, 106; in sleep, 87
Immediacy: elements of, 17; eroticism in, 18

Immortality, 60, 141; unspeakability of, 141–142
the Imperative, 121–127
Imperialism, 149; of meaning, 100
Impressions, 19–24, 23; body of, 23; cognitively endowed, 24; consciousness of, 15, 17; deterioration of, 39; fullness of, 18; ideas derived from, 33; lapsing of, 40; memory of, 42; production from, 15; and thought, 21; transience of, 17; unproductive, 25
Indifference: prejudices of, xii; safety of, xi
Induction, 53
Infinity, 42, 70
Initiation, 61–62, 121–127; and body praxis, xi; guidance of, ix
Inner: exigence, 7; gaze, 9; listening, 12–18; speech, 10–12
Inquiry (Hume), 13–14, 15
Instruments, 3–18
Intellect: achievements of, 22; blank in, 4, 6; death of, 21; and discontinuity, 6; disruption in, 33; focus of, 24, 34; and foresight, 33; grasping of, 5; hegemony of, 69; inner circuit of, 12; light of, 54; objectifying function of, 6; perpetuating, 24; and privation, 15; productive, 18, 26, 29, 34; refocus of, 46; regeneration of, 21; rest state of, 56; retentive stance of, 34; sameness of, 30; and somatic awareness, 51; speech of, xii; threats to power of, 6
Intellectualism, xii, xiii
Intention, amnesia of, 3
the Interval, 79–85
Intuition, 28
Irony, 112

K
Kant, Immanuel, 24, 25, 26, 28, 29, 33, 39, 40, 46, 65, 67, 72, 84, 103–104, 106, 108, 111, 119, 121, 122, 125, 134, 141, 147, 153, 156
Kierkegaard, Søren, 107
Kinaesthesis, 13, 25, 53, 59, 63, 93
Knowledge: constrained, 4; of dependencies, 48; effect of blank on, 13; empirical, 25; empowerment of, 10; genuine, 32; human, 124–125; intellectual, 27, 112; limits of, 32; and memory, 47; objects of, 15, 25–26; obligation, 63; past, 4; a priori, 25; privative, 17, 132; problems of, xi; production, 15, 19, 30, 32; of pure existence, 31; restriction of, ix; sameness of, ix; self, 63, 125; and sensation, 27; sexual, 18; of signs, 108; and thanatos, 17; theory of, xiii; through reason, 52; through senses, 52

L
Language, 25; and the blank, 10; conscience in, 147; and discourse, 12; of displacement, 49; double meanings in, 99; of essence, 97; essential of, 12; objective, 93; ontological, ix; of pathology, 35; preexisting, 98–99; of Vedanta, 30
Lethe, 80; and meaning, 100; and presence, 113
Liberation, 30
Listening: inner, 12–18; selfless, 126
Locke, John, 1, 4, 5, 6, 7, 9, 10, 11, 13, 21, 22, 30, 31–32, 39, 40, 46, 47, 53, 80, 87, 90, 91, 106, 115

Logic: of choice, 16; empirical, 58; of equality, 57; intellectual, 58; of productivity, 15; of sameness, 60; of self-interest, 132; somatic, 58; tenets of, 59
Logos: conflict with, 107; of privation, 132; somatic, 57, 58, 92, 99, 104, 107, 139, 158; of suffering, 50, 131, 132
Loss, 17
Love, 161; birth of, xii; dialectic of, 81, 111; obligation of, 109; seeking, 109; self, 83, 84–85; and Strife, 80, 81
Lumen naturale, 69, 160; abolishment of difference in, 28; of intellect, 54; of understanding, 27

M
Marcel, Gabriel, 45, 46, 47, 53, 54, 58, 59, 63, 64, 66, 100, 115, 142
Marginalization, 6, 81; of dilemmas, 142
Meaning, 87–94; absence of, 12; assignment to class, 90; awareness of, 104; ceremony of, 124; communication of, 47; conceptual, 13; of death, 84–85; designation of, 97; of disruption, 29; essential, 93, 95, 112; of the ethical, 141; intellectual, 24; in language, 99; and lethe, 100; of meaning, 100, 103; as measure of being, 122; protection of, 113; in recurrence of correspondence, 93; representational theory of, 4; safeguarding of, 125; search for, 109; signification of consciousness in, 87; and subjectivity, 100; synonomous, 88; in thought, 3
Meditations (Descartes), 82, 87
Memory: alien, 141; ambiguity of, 138; ambitiousness of, 138; anarchical, 157; bearing of, 137; and the blank, 21; charge of, 87; and conscience, x–xi; in consciousness, xii; of correspondence, 94; deterioration of impressions in, 39; displaced, 9; disrupted, 35, 37, 92; embodiment of, 59; empowerment of knowledge in, 10; failure of, 5; of humanity's purpose, 160; and imagination, 13, 42; immemorable, 96, 106, 113, 123, 133; immemorial, 80; of impressions, 42; incomplete, 139; as interior gazing, 4; and knowledge, 47; lapses in, 135; overstressed, 17; of the past, 52; patient, 137; perfect, 87; presentational, 42; presumptive, 139; reinforcement of, 113; remembering the immemorial, 59; retentive, 4, 6, 7, 11; return of, 46; safeguarding freedom of, vii; and sameness, 39; somatic, 59; the stop disguised as, 47; strength of, 88; surpassing, 156; suspension of, 82; and sympathy, 135; and time, 83; transmission of, x; traumatic, 82; and the unmemorable, 21; weakening of, 88, 89; weightless weight of, 135
Metanoia, 13
Mill, John Stuart, 125
Mind: blank of, 3–10, 9; faculties of, 5; image of, 52, 106; productive, 21; property-making, 31; and retention, 5, 30; tentive character of, 4, 13, 14, 31, 51, 56
Mortality, 141
Movement, 17, 61; actuality of, 30; alteration of consciousness of, 58; of the body, 56; choice of,

Movement *(continued)*
21; and consciousness, 58, 63, 159; deadened, 56; of energy, 25; local, 25; recollective, 47; self-sufficient system of, 25; setting thought in, xii–xiii; somatic, xi, 25, 34; of time, 39, 40, 139; transition to, 35–74; unadorned, 22

N

Nature: appropriation of property from, 11; conflict in, 7; discovery of, 96; of fear, 44; state of, 7, 21; uniformity of, 39
Nichtdasein, 132, 140
Nietzsche, Friedrich, xiii, 19, 21, 90
Nihilism, xiii, 79
Nominalism, 92
Nondisclosure, 111–117

O

Obedience: absolute, 160; agreement of, 156; choiceless, 157; and effort, 159; enigma of, x; forgotten, xii; paradox of, 159; reduction to, 157; replacement of, ix; and transmission of memory, x
Objectification, 13, 52
Objectivity, 87–94; burden of subjectivity in, 91; and essentialism, 93; liberation by, 91; project of, 75; quantification of being in, 91; self-view of, 90–91
Obligation, 62, 65, 100; acceptance of, 83–84; answering to, 117; awareness of, 147; binding, 126; discharge of, 68; discontinuity of, 68; double, 126, 138; of the ego, 81; ethical, viii; heeding, 129; initiation into, 84, 101; knowledge of, 63; of love, 109; signification by, 116; and subjectivity, 147, 148; uncreated, 62
Obscurity, 46
Obsession, xi
"Of Retention" (Locke), 4
"Of the Imperfection of Words" (Locke), 11
"Of the Origin of Ideas" (Hume), 21
On Memory and Reminiscence (Aristotle), 4
Ontology: bracketing of, vii; disruption of, 116, 117; failure of, 115; language of, ix; of object consciousness, 49; and preservation of signification, 113; as shelter, 113, 114; and suffering, 131
Optics, 32
Optics (Euclid), 32
Origination of origination, viii
the Other: command of, viii; disruptive, ix, x; exchange with, x, xii; in-time, 44; separateness of, xi; suffering of, 68; uplifting of, viii

P

Paracelsus, 92–93, 96, 97, 99, 104, 108
Paradox: of obedience, 159; of retained retention, 43
Pathology: and disruption, 48; invitation to, 57; language of, 35; symptomology in, 49; as three-fold deformation, 48; treatment of, 49
Perception, xiii, 18; and anarchaic function, 34; and cognition, xiii, 28; conceptually unendowed, 27; and consciousness, 60; and difference, 22; and exchange,

60; existential, 28; of form, 24; formless, 24–30; of the formless, 24–30; informing by, 47; linear, 32; "lively," 61; nirvikalpanic, 30–31; original of, 21; of present impressions, 4; productive, 25; self-constituting, 104; of senses, 16; sympathetic, 61, 62, 94; theories of, 105; visayagatic, 30–31
Percipience, 63, 65, 83, 99, 124; action of, 61; and active imagination, 104; as altered consciousness, 52; blinded, 51; character of, 59; constitution of, 52; disruption of, 64; initiatory, 61; power of, 92; and relaity, 65; and subjectivity, 124; and temporal presence, 61
Perfection, 138
Perspective, linear, 6
The Phenomenology of Internal Time-Consciousness (Husserl), 40
Physics (Aristotle), 55
Plato, xiii, 18
Positivism, 89
Poverty: fear of, 5–6; as idol, 142; and retention, 5
Power: anarchaic, 141; of the blank, 13; borrowing, 141; of conscience, 158; of disease, 50; disruptive, 84; impoverishment of, 5; intellectual, 6, 52; invisible, 62; of *lumen naturale*, 27; of object consciousness, 19; of percipience, 92; of recollection, 4; of revelation, 114; transformative, 50
Praxis, 137–143, 160; body, xi
Precedence, viii
Predestination, 113
Preservation, 5
Proclus, 84–85, 94, 95
Production: of consciousness, vii, 46; control of, 15; from impressions, 15; intellectual, 1, 26, 29, 34; of knowledge, 15, 19, 30, 32; machinery of, 61; necessity of, 12; nonstop, 26; and object consciousness, 1; of objects of knowledge, 15; of thought, 21; of words, 12
Projection, xi
Property, 5; appropriation from nature, 11; personal, 5
Proprioception, 53
Protention, 52
Psychopathology of Everyday Life (Freud), 9

R

Rage, sacred, 112
Reaction, 21
Reality: awareness of, 7; sense of, 26; unveiling of, 65, 111
Reason: absence of, 133; antinomy of, 134; hegemony of, 7; knowledge through, 52; lack of, 17; pure, 125, 134; rules of, 58
Redemption, 19; and disruption, vii
Reflection, 46; point of, 8*fig*
Representation, 15, 21
Resemblance, 16
Responsibility, 83; authorlessness of, 131; choice in, viii, 123; command to, viii; comprehension of, 130, 131; and conscience, 147; of consciousness, 119; and decision, 122; of disclosure, 124–125; evasion of, 142; for naming of self, 93; noncoincidence of, 145; release to, 154; replacement of, ix
Retention, 5, 9, 16, 17, 19; and anarchaic function, 21; continuity of, 42, 47; economy of, 5;

Retention *(continued)*
and entropy, 35; of the forbidden, 10; and the gaze, 16, 24, 54; hegemony of, 21; and meeting being, 49; neutralization of, 19; and poverty, 5; as prevention, 42; reclaiming attention from, 46; and sameness, 39; self-containment of, 52; somatic critique of, 45–50; and subjectivity, 66; and temporality, 43, 82; and tension, 48; and wealth, 5
Reticence, 53
"Running off phenomena," 40, 44, 46, 50, 57, 60, 80, 84–85; modification of, 40–41
Russell, Bertrand, 88, 107

S

Sadness, 115
Sameness: alteration of, 43; illusions of, 80; of intellect, 30, 40; of knowledge, ix; logic of, 60; and memory, 39; and object consciousness, 23; and retention, 39; of soma, 30; temporality of, 57
Self: absorption, 46; destruction, 90; eroticism, 83; examination, 46; identity, 61, 84; interest, xi, 92, 140; knowledge, 63, 125; limitation, 65; will, 103
Sensations: anticipation of, 25; description of, 39; disrupted, 29; Enlightenment concept of, 22; episodic, 29; and intellectual knowledge, 27; unadorned, 22
Sensitivity, 7, 15
Shadowing, 53
Signification, 111; discovery of, 79; displacement of, 87; of disruption, xii; by essence, 148; ethical, 148; expansion of, 112; and human acts, vii; by obligation, 116; permenence of, 141; preservation of, 113; sacrifice in, 141; self-enclosing of, 106; significance of, vii; and subjectivity, 99; of suffering, 154–155; by sympathy, 97
Silence, 148; of speech, 11
"Sinking down," 40, 42, 60, 80
Sleep, 87, 117
Socrates, 125, 151
Solipsism, 94
Soma: alteration of, xi; awareness of, xi, 27; disruptiveness of, 33–34; energy in, 27, 53, 140; the gaze on, 47; glimpsing, 27; logos of, 57, 58, 92, 99, 104, 107, 158; movement of, 25; rigidification in, 49; sameness of, 30; spatial relations of, 69; tangibility of, 53; vigilance toward, 47; vulnerability of, 49
Space: conception of, 31, 33; continuity in, 58; coordinates in, 32; and disruption, 129; Euclidean, 32; of geometry, 28; in-becoming, 70; independence from objects in, 31, 32; intellectual, 32–33; inversion of, 72; optical, 72; projective, 72, 74; pure, 70; between thoughts, 59; three-dimensional, 6; as transparency, 28; visual, 28, 32, 69, 72
Space-time continuum, vii, x
Speech: to consciousness, 108; of essence, 98; exterior, 98; inner, 10–12, 13, 21, 22; necessity of, 12; silence of, 11; of sympathy, 108
Spinoza, Benedict de, xi, 115, 131
Spontaneity, 44
Stoicism, xiii
the Stop: in automaticity, 45; disguised as memory, 47; inner

speech and, 22; institution of, 123; and intellectual production, 34; neutralization of, 19; reclaiming attention from retention, 46; retentivity in, 51; sacred hush of, 84–85
Subjectivity, 48; and arche name *I*, 67; autonomous, 153; as burden to objectivity, 91; closure of, 107; and conscience, 108; and consciousness, 57, 65; defining, 57; development of, x; disclosure of the sign in, 98; disruptive element of, 106; and ego, 93; enlargement of, 59; and essence, 95, 98, 112, 125; ethics in, 100, 130; gap in, viii; and geocentrism, 69; as inequality, 93; interior of, 134; and meaning, 95, 100, 103; and obligation, 147, 148; origin of, 121; and passivity, 130; patience of, 133; and percipience, 124; potency of, 140; potential for guidance, 157; potentization of, 140; reach of, 67; reduction to obedience, 157; and retention, 66; self-aggrandizement of, 121; and signification, 99; in subposition, 103; and substitution, 89, 90; summons to, viii; surpassing of, 154; and sympathy, 125; transformation of, 131; trial of, 145; vulnerability of, 122; and will, 15, 66
Subjugation, 6
Subservience, 129
Succussion, 140
Suffering, 63, 83, 133; alien, 154; alteration of, 131; disruption of, 101; ethical, 101, 131; as greater good, 117; incomprehension in, 130; knowledge of, 105–106; logos of, 131, 132; making one's own, 117; passivity in, 129–135, 131; signification of, 154–155; taking on the other's, 157; transformation of, 131
Suicide, 123
Summons, 119–158
Sympathy: all-suffering of, 63; and awareness, xiii; and consciousness, 104; demands of, 63; eradication of, 48; and essence, 97, 103; manifestation through, 98; and memory, 135; of openness, 100; pathos of, 100; and perception, 61, 62, 94; and plight of self, 95–101; signification by, 97; speech of, 108; spirit of, 21; and subjectivity, 125; unfulfilled, 116
Symposium (Socrates), 151

T

Temporality: altered, 44; reappearance of, 80; and retention, 43
Tension, xiii; and retention, 48
Tentivity, 4, 5, 9
Thanatos, 9, 17
Thought: and anger, 112; as ascesis, 10; birth of, xii, 1; as celibacy, 10; communication of, 12; and concealment, 19; confines of, 33; directed, 112; discharge of, 10; discursive, 112; dissemination of, 10; economy of, 15; enervation of, 1; existence of, xiv, 19; and impression, 16, 21; inferiority to impression, 14–15; inferiority to sensation, 17; meaning of, 3; meeting, xii; order of, xii; organization of, xii; productive, 21; and rage, 112; recording, 11; redirection of, 46; relatedness of, xiv; space between, 19, 59; stoppage in, 3
Timaeus, 81

Time: in altered consciousness, 61; being in, 27, 29, 34; bracketed, 84–85; consciousness, 39–44; continuity in, 43, 44, 58; deliverance of, 95; of difference, 82; dimensions of, 40; and disruption, 129; equalities of, 81; of healing, 83; immemorable, 61; internal, xiii, 39–44; and intuition, 82; maintenance of, 43; making, 51; and memory, 83; movement of, 39, 40, 139; nonlinear, 9; other-in, 44; participation in, 61; persistance in, 81; remaking, 43; retention of, 82; running off of, 80; of self-constitution, 82; stop of, 41; traumatized, 82; withdrawal of, 80; wounded, 83
Traditionalism, xii
Transcendentalism, 24, 125
Transformation, 75–117
Transparency, xiii, 58, 63, 70, 132, 133; of autonomy, 134; combustion of, 160; creation of, 54; and disruption, 28; and distance, 69; ego's dream of, 159; of the frame, 25; of horizon, vii; indifference of, 28; of space, 28; of visual world, 28
Treatise of Government (Locke), 5
Truth: concealed, 82; feigning of, 111
Twinning, 23–24

U

Upanishads, 30–31
Utilitarianism, xiii, 125

V

Vanishing point, 8*fig*, 9, 32, 72
the Veil, 32; mystery of, 124; and vision, 32; vulnerability of, 115
Vulnerability: of consciousness, 75; disruption of, 115; and immediacy, 116; and patience, 137; somatic, 49; of subjectivity, 122; of veiling, 115

W

Wealth, 5
Will: autonomous, 81, 82; ethical, 81; hyperextention of, 130; obligations of, 81; overreaching of, 55; and refusal, 42; resumption of, 81; self, 103; and subjectivity, 15, 66; submission of, 66

9782625R00112

Printed in Great Britain
by Amazon.co.uk, Ltd.,
Marston Gate.